*Penguin Books*

# Down and Out

Sandy Craig was born in 1949 and graduated from Edinburgh University in 1971 with a first class honours M.A. in philosophy and English literature. In 1971 he helped John McGrath start the 7:84 Theatre Company and for most of the next five years he worked in alternative theatre. In 1976 he became a freelance journalist. He was a member of the Arts Council's Drama Panel from 1978–80 and edited *Dreams and Deconstructions: Alternative Theatre in Britain* (1980). In 1981 he helped start the London magazine *City Limits* and was its first Chairperson. He has worked for *City Limits*, the *Listener*, the *Sunday Times* and the *Radio Times*, among other publications. He is married with a baby daughter.

Chris Schwarz was born in London in 1948. He started working as a photographer in Japan in 1970. He returned to England the following year after travelling overland from Japan to London. After this he became photographer-in-residence for the Combination at the Albany, Deptford. Since 1973 he has worked as a freelance photographer. Among his exhibitions are 'Inside Whitechapel' (1973); 'Homeless' (1974); 'The People of Dartington' (1975–7); 'Seven Dancers' (1978); 'London Calling . . .' (1980–81), a touring exhibition on the problems experienced by young unemployed people coming to London; and 'Our Neighbours' (1982), a portrait of Hammersmith commissioned by the Riverside Studios. His other work includes a photo documentary on the Shakers of New England and a film *Other Rooms*. In 1982 he won the GLC photographic competition 'Metropolis: Portrait of a City' for pictures from 'London Calling . . .'

# Down and Out

ORWELL'S PARIS AND LONDON REVISITED

TEXT BY SANDY CRAIG AND PHOTOGRAPHS BY CHRIS SCHWARZ

PENGUIN BOOKS

Penguin Books Ltd, Harmondsworth, Middlesex, England
Penguin Books, 40 West 23rd Street, New York, New York 10010, U.S.A.
Penguin Books Australia Ltd, Ringwood, Victoria, Australia
Penguin Books Canada Ltd, 2801 John Street, Markham, Ontario, Canada L3R 1B4
Penguin Books (N.Z.) Ltd, 182–190 Wairau Road, Auckland 10, New Zealand

First published 1984

Made and Printed in Great Britain by
Butler & Tanner Ltd, Frome and London

Filmset in 11/13 Sabon

Designed by David Grogan

# *Preface*

Fifty years ago as I write, George Orwell's autobiographical documentary *Down and Out in Paris and London* was published. In Paris he led the impecunious life of the bohemian and struggling writer. His savings were stolen and, with poverty staring him in the face, he searched for work, eventually finding casual employment as a *plongeur*, an exhausting combination of dishwasher and skivvy. Worn out, he got a friend in London to pay his passage back and find him work in England, only to discover on arrival that the job had been delayed a month. Ashamed to rely too much on his friend's generosity he eked out the month in the underworld of seedy lodging-houses, Salvation Army hostels and the government casual ward, or 'spike', in the company of beggars and tramps.

Much of the world that Orwell described is relatively unchanged today. True, there is no longer the widespread domestic poverty, and working conditions for those in the worst jobs may be less infernal. Orwell's *plongeur*, if he has the good fortune to work in one of the few Paris restaurants, which, because of their size, are regularly inspected by the authorities, today has some protection over his security, conditions of work and pay. There are shorter hours, and there is kitchen technology – bread-slicing machines, waste-disposal units, electric industrial dishwashers – to help him. But the hotel and restaurant hierarchy remains unaltered: the *plongeur* is still the lowest of the low. And the work is still done by immigrants, usually these days either Arabs or Africans.

The difference and the improvements in conditions would surely have struck Orwell less forcibly than the extraordinary lack of change during those fifty years. This revisit intersperses sections of Orwell's text with contemporary descriptions. What is remarkable is that whole sections of Sandy Craig's text could be replaced by Orwell's, and vice versa. Even the places are the same. If George Orwell were alive he might walk into Bruce House from the unfamiliarly fashionable Covent Garden and feel as if he had never been away. The hostel remains, like others, steadfastly locked into the Victorian ethos of the workhouse, the same as it always was but for an additional fifty years of grime and delapidation.

It is not just the buildings themselves which remain unchanged. Attitudes to homeless people have altered depressingly little. The way the hostels are administered, the rules which are a further burden to the already humiliating lives of the hostel inmates, still seem designed to transform ordinary people with conventional aspirations into the dossers of our imagination.

To some extent it was difficult for Orwell, as it is for observers of this scene today, to avoid confirming those images of homeless people as a race apart. The bright lights of the city centre highlight for us the miserable quality of life which many people have to endure, but they may also produce distorting effects. The accounts of the drink, drugs and prostitution that pervade the lives of many of the homeless people described in this book are not exaggerated. Yet if we become too fascinated by such horrors, we may be distracted from the most important features of the individuals whose words and pictures fill these pages. And, more importantly, the reader may reassure himself that the foreignness of such experience is further confirmation of how far removed from his own world are the people here described, for whom he may feel pity but no sense of identification.

'Dossers', 'junkies', 'down and outs', 'queers', 'delinquents': the list of labels in English or in French is almost endless, and each label helps us to distance ourselves from the people we encounter in this book. Some of the labels, particularly among the young, may be self-imposed but they serve our purpose equally well. A homeless youth may trouble our consciences; a punk or a *zonard* is disturbing in quite a different way, almost inviting a negative and uncomprehending response.

One perhaps curious feature of this alternative cityscape is that here we find a handful of people who are, in fact, very much present by choice. True, the alternative available to people, like Tam and Dave, the Scotsmen turned Parisian beggars, may seem pretty bleak but still they feel to some extent in control and able to get out if and when they want to. That they are, in this respect, unusual would have been no argument for excluding such people from the book. These characters provide a more explicit comment than many others on the opportunities – or lack of them – offered by our society to resourceful and imaginative people. They reject mainstream society not because they see themselves as part of a movement for social change, but because they cannot conceive of a social change which would include them in that mainstream.

But though Tam and Dave may be in the minority of those who consciously reject society, this does not mean that the other people described in the book have lost their individuality. In their attitudes, their ways of coping with the material and other deprivations which they face, and in the extent to which their spirit has been broken by those deprivations, they are extraordinarily varied. And it is as well that the often eccentric and colourful personalities of the individuals who have chosen this way of life can also distract our attention from the reality of life without a home or job.

Yet in one crucial respect all but a very few of the people in this book –

indeed all but a very few homeless people in the major cities – are in a similar position: there is simply no possibility for these people of identifying any option realistically open to them which would leave them in circumstances considered remotely tolerable by most people in our still wealthy Western society.

This point needs the greatest possible emphasis. As the story of each of the men and women portrayed in the text unfolds, it is instructive to ask ourselves what, practically, we would have them do to extract themselves from the cycle of homelessness and lack of work. Any honest appraisal must end in the conclusion that no realistic escape route exists.

The aspirations of the great majority of homeless people are predictable and conventional. All they want is somewhere with a degree of independence, security and privacy, and a pretty modest degree of comfort. Some of them may no longer be able to manage in entirely unsupported accommodation after years in which their dignity, self-respect and ability to cope have been systematically undermined by an environment where such qualities are worthless and indeed may heighten the bitterness and humiliation of the situation in which they find themselves.

If the almost total lack of progress in improving the conditions of many hostels is the most depressing feature of this book when set against Orwell's, perhaps the most disturbing aspect is the accurate observation of the growth, especially in the last few years, of homelessness among young people, a phenomenon not recorded at all by Orwell. Partly, this reflects the appearance of a whole generation of adolescents and young adults who seem to have no function in society. Unemployment and, even worse, the lack of any prospects of employment, bring specific stresses for individuals and for families and it can be no surprise that, as a consequence, large numbers of young people leave home searching for opportunities to give their lives some sense of purpose.

But the growth of young homelessness in Britain, for example, also directly reflects a failure in the British housing system. Private rented accommodation has almost entirely disappeared. Single people are generally excluded from council housing both by the excess of demand over supply and by the failure of local authorities to perceive single people as being in need of housing. As a result there is little chance of renting somewhere to live. This is made worse by a government which devotes all its energy and resources to the promotion of a form of tenure, owner-occupation, which is quite obviously a non-starter for homeless people. The result is that there are perhaps fewer opportunities for young people seeking accommodation than there have ever been in the past.

This book concentrates on youth homelessness in the centre of two capital cities. It accurately describes individuals whose previous family and neighbourhood support networks have, in most cases, irrevocably broken down. But away from the special conditions of Piccadilly and Earl's Court there is a much larger number of young people who have not yet migrated from their home territory but who have nowhere secure to call home, who live semi-itinerant lives, sleeping on friends' floors, occasionally relying on hostels, sometimes trying to put up with a few days back in unsatisfactory family conditions.

This phenomenon is evident even within the inner city. In Southwark, just a mile or two from the West End of London, there were 663 cases of young homeless in one year, of whom 90 per cent were local youths. The minority of those young people who come from the provinces to London do so because they can no longer in any way rely on family and friends locally. They do so because no specialized agencies exist in most of our smaller towns or cities to provide advice and guidance to a young person seeking somewhere to live, so that at the point at which a deteriorating relationship with the family finally breaks down the pressure to move to the big city is greatly increased.

In all Western societies people are seeking independence earlier; single-person households are becoming common and therefore the average household size has been decreasing. But far from developing new policies to respond to those changes, we seem to have erected new barriers for single people seeking homes. Our highly mobile society presents no adequate route for young working-class people to progress from dependence on family to an independent life.

This is not the case for many more fortunate young people who, for example, undertake higher education. At best, they will live in a college or hall of residence, with meals provided. At worst, skilled people, well informed about available accommodation in the area, will be on hand to advise and assist and to ensure that they get access to the dwindling supply of private rented accommodation.

For many other young people the issue can be postponed, even if they would wish it otherwise, until they are married or at least somewhat older. But for a substantial minority this option does not exist and while it may be of some interest to inquire why this is so, the interest is largely academic. That it is and will be necessary for many young people to seek to form their first household at eighteen or nineteen years of age is an unremarkable fact which requires a practical response.

An obvious and generally understandable response to this assertion is to feel that young people should stay at home. Indeed, the advice of most young homeless people to their contemporaries is, as a rule: Don't leave home unless you have to. But many do have to, assuming they have a home in the first place. These include, on the one hand, the 8,000 children who leave care each year and, on the other, those people like the Scots lad who came to Shelter, whose departure from home was heralded by his father burning his mattress in the back garden.

But just as the horror stories of those who are 'down and out' may distract us from an analysis of why these phenomena occur, so too much emphasis on family breakdown, unemployment or any other social condition may obscure the fact that the wish to be independent, to leave home, to see something more of the world than your own economically rundown town is entirely natural and is often thought of as admirable. The exhortation to people to 'get on your bike and look for work' always seemed a particularly harsh one, but never more so than for the people who respond only to be told they should have stayed at home.

We all, at some stage, *need* housing – when we first look for an independent place to live. For those for whom renting, rather than buying, is the only option, the obstacles are much greater. Effectively they are told that simply requiring somewhere to live is not enough. That ordinary need must be supplemented by some personal inadequacy or failure before it will be classified as real need.

In Britain, what this means for those fortunate enough to be considered a priority for council housing – principally families with children and pensioners – is that they are required to reach a crisis in their lives before being eligible for housing. Irrevocable family breakdown, violence within the family, severe physical or mental illness – only, it seems, when people are beset by such problems does the State begin to respond.

For single people even these conditions will generally not be sufficient because of the way in which we organize our housing. Small wonder that in one Home Counties area, nine out of ten young women who have been in local authority care as children become pregnant within a year of leaving care, aged eighteen or even less. The phenomenon causes great excitement in the press: 'Council official tells girl: Get pregnant if you want a house.' Yet again the petty salaciousness of the story and the implicit condemnation of the local official help to hide the simple truth. Getting pregnant can be a way to a home, sometimes the only one, and the local official who gives an eighteen-year-old girl that information is doing no more than the job requires.

The picture is not uniformly bleak. The Welfare State, at least for the time being, does exist and it provides protection which was not available in the 1930s. Indeed, the availability of a guaranteed income from the Department of Health and Social Security has created a small new service industry of landlords providing accommodation in multi-occupied houses throughout the country.

These are the temporary lodging-places of the invisible homeless: those people living with no security either of home or generally of permanent employment, for whom the institutions of the Welfare State, notably the Health Service, are difficult to gain access to. Occupants of such accommodation are almost ten times more likely than their fellow citizens to die in one of the fires that regularly rage through these anonymous lodging-houses.

It is true that this state of affairs exists for the same reason as the growth in young homelessness has occurred. But if the failure to provide a means by which young people can move towards independence has been partly a failure of imagination, the wider failure to deal with the needs of single homeless people generally is more culpable. The needs of single people are well documented. Single people account for more than one in four of the population and while our population has been static the rise in the number of households has been a widely discussed feature of recent census returns.

This is not to say that we know exactly how many single homeless people there are. Precisely because this is an area of provision with which the State has never felt it had to concern itself, it ignores in large measure the very existence of single homeless people. Such people approaching local authorities are often not only turned away, but their application is not even noted. In many areas single people cannot even get on to waiting lists, still less get rehoused from such lists.

At a national level the needs of the single homeless and the pressure on accommodation seem deliberately to be played down. The Department of the Environment assumes, for the purpose of constructing housing plans, that 75 per cent of single people who share accommodation do so willingly. Yet the Department's own survey of 'sharers' found that two thirds of those people would prefer to have an independent, self-contained place to live.

What is certain is that tens of thousands of single people are without a home in London every night. Most accurate estimates suggest a total of 14,000 people in hostels, many others sleeping rough, or otherwise without somewhere to live. And in Paris the authors' decision to use Orwell's *Down and Out in Paris and London* as a starting-point for a re-examination of the conditions he had observed, coincided with the Salvation Army in that city deciding that it was necessary for them to begin their soup-run again for the first time since Orwell's day.

The numbers are startling and should surely shock even those who feel that the city centres of our two capitals are bound to be inhabited by some itinerants who will never be caught by even the most sophisticated safety net. Moreover, the numbers are equally shocking in Britain's provincial towns and cities. All Shelter's twenty Housing Aid Centres report steadily increasing numbers of single homeless people, and newspaper articles confirming this impression are an almost daily feature.

In Bedford, for example, an English county district of 130,000 inhabitants in the comparatively affluent South, it is reported by local police that on any given night 100 people, most of them young, may be sleeping rough. There is absolutely no reason to suppose that the figures for Bedford are exceptional and this, in turn, would seem to suggest that altogether a terrifying 40,000 young people may be homeless in Britain.

It is a most appropriate time to look at these trends in an international context. Other Western cities, most notably in the United States, are reporting steep increases in 'hobos', 'bums', 'clochards', 'barboni' – the labels change from country to country. In the United States, too, they seem to be leading the way in rejecting any attempt to assist the homeless, preferring instead to pass local bye-laws which impose stiff penalties for vagrancy and push the problem on to the next community. It is surely one of the most profound moral failures of Western societies that having been so nearly successful in protecting their citizens from absolute poverty they immediately, when faced with a threat to that material wealth, consign those at the margins back into real deprivation rather than reducing the resources available to those who are the most wealthy.

It is part of the thesis on which this book is based that the need of the single homeless people encountered in Paris and London cannot practically be met except as part of a general improvement in housing conditions for the homeless and badly housed. None the less, in Britain at least it is still worthwhile looking at ways of assisting single homeless people as a specific group, largely because the rejection until now of single people in need of housing means that there are many short-term measures which can be taken.

CHAR, the Campaign for Single Homeless People, is the agency with the most outstanding record of promoting the rights of the sort of people represented in this book. It began life ten years ago as the Campaign for the Homeless and Rootless – hence CHAR – but realized after some years in the field that the use of the word 'rootless' in the name created in the minds of the public the image of the vagrant, the *clochard*, the dosser, when CHAR's clients tended to be people desperate to end their involuntary mobility.

CHAR's manifesto, 'Local Housing for Single People', is the most thorough exposition of how we can ensure that the next fifty years bring more improvement than the last in the lives of single people on low, variable incomes.

The CHAR blueprint rightly begins by pointing out that the very refusal in many areas to consider the housing needs of single people as a legitimate cause for concern effectively obscures those needs. It suggests, too, that a willingness to end those policies which prevent the entry of single people on to the waiting list or fail even to log the fact that a single homeless person has asked the council for help, would be substantial progress in itself.

One of the factors which make people reluctant to give homeless single people access to conventional housing is the assumption that most men, in particular, could not cope with independent living after years and sometimes (in the case of, say, someone who spent their childhood in care and then joined the army) a lifetime in institutions of one kind or another.

In fact those authorities which have taken the trouble to test their own assumptions have found they were badly wrong. In Glasgow the District Council found that three quarters of single homeless people were able to be rehoused with no more than the usual assistance given to new tenants. Indeed, of 500 single men from hostels rehoused in the city, 90 per cent were still in their flats with no more than the average management problems after two years.

Of course, there are special requirements to be considered. Many single people need furnished accommodation and a minority will need a certain amount of extra support for some time after they are rehoused. In Glasgow, once again, this has been made possible by the council employing six 'Home-makers' who help people who are not able to live entirely independently. In other cases, more conventional solutions involving the use of residential wardens may be necessary.

One of the most important characteristics of all the intelligent attempts to improve conditions for the hostel-dwellers of Britain's cities has been the reduction in size of these hostels. In this they are in marked contrast to the institutions most frequently referred to in this book. Arlington House has over 1,000 beds, the Camberwell Reception Centre 985, Bruce House 600, as well, of course, as the enormous 'prison of the hungry' in Paris known to Orwell during his time as a 'down and out'. There are many others; for example Salvation Army hostels, where bed spaces exceed 100 and where the sleeping accommodation is in dormitories. It is really not possible to conceive of such places providing a home that is in any way tolerable, however liberal and enlightened its managers. This has now been recognized and in some of these institutions bed spaces are being reduced, but progress is slow.

The fact that such institutions still exist adds piquancy to a dilemma faced by Orwell and which is still very much in the forefront of political arguments about the single homeless today. Orwell himself attacked the London County Council for closing substandard hostels and thereby leaving men who relied on those hostels with no roof at all over their heads.

The danger that the best may be the enemy of the good, in so far as the adjective 'good' can be applied to rotten accommodation, because it is preferable to sleeping rough, continues to be frequently cited as a reason for inaction. Early in 1983, after years of pressure from CHAR, Shelter and others, a Private Member's Bill was put before Parliament which would have introduced certain minimum standards into houses in multiple occupation. Almost the sole argument of substance raised against the Bill was that it would result in the closure of establishments which would not be replaced. Sadly the Bill fell as a result of the General Election.

Although we should be wary of those who suggest that it is in the interests of the homeless – in the short term, naturally – to stay in hostels in which most people would not last one night, none the less there is a real dilemma. This dilemma is surely best resolved by the homeless themselves.

They can decide what is acceptable short-term accommodation, even if substandard, and what has gone beyond the bounds of acceptability. This happened in 1981 at the abominable Bruce House when residents decided that they could no longer tolerate the conditions and, with the support of CHAR and the local law centre, successfully took legal action against Westminster City Council to get the hostel improved.

There is, in any case, no possible justification for the refusal of urban authorities to draw up plans for the closure of large, substandard and dangerous hostels. A voluntary agency, struggling to cope with an immediate night-by-night need, may feel under an obligation to keep open a substandard hostel, but it is reasonable to expect local councils to think further ahead.

The assumption that the State need only concern itself with the needs of people who cannot help themselves, such as children and the elderly, will no longer do. It is not incumbent on the State to provide housing directly for all its citizens but it is necessary for it to ensure that sufficient housing is available and to provide the last-resort housing, at the very least. This task exists just as surely for single people as for anyone else.

The idea that people who are denied access to a home or a job are being denied basic human rights is no longer fashionable, and perhaps rightly so. A more relevant concept, developed by David Donnison, former head of the Supplementary Benefits Commission, is that of 'rights of citizenship'. The lack of a secure home is perhaps the greatest obstacle to participating in our society. Without a home, a job is more difficult to come by, adequate health care is a problem, credit is generally impossible to obtain, voting rights are often lost. It is remarkable the extent to which a place of residence is a condition of citizenship, and 'no fixed abode' a label which consigns people to a wholly inferior status.

It follows that a society which fails to make available to its citizens the opportunity of a home of a quality commensurate with the wealth of that society, has no right to expect those people whom it fails to fulfil *their* obligations and responsibilities as citizens. Providing for every citizen the opportunity of somewhere decent to live will not end the drug and alcohol abuse and the prostitution which is a feature of the lives of many of the people described in this book, but any sensible analysis of those problems must conclude that there is no hope of reducing their incidence while homelessness afflicts a growing number of people.

Those in authority can count themselves fortunate that most of the people deprived of 'rights of citizenship' still somehow manage to fulfil their part of this social contract. While this is the case, the rest of us can continue to turn a blind eye to the blighted lives around us. But if more people, particularly among the young, turn from resignation to a bitter rejection of what they rightly perceive to be a very one-sided bargain we will all have to live with the consequences.

Neil McIntosh
Director of Shelter

# Authors' note

Orwell's account is based on his own first-hand experience. We approached our subjects as journalists, introducing ourselves as such. By far the great majority of the photographs were taken with the subjects' knowledge and consent. In the writing, some events have been transposed, others emphasized. It should not be assumed that the *characters* described in the text necessarily bear any resemblance to the *people* shown in the photographs: written text and photographic text have different functions, and the written text employs techniques – the use of statistics, political analysis, introspection and fictional devices – which are not available to photography. We hope that this will complement the naturalistic account of 'life with the down-and-outs' (who are only one category of the homeless) with empirical findings and the beginnings of a structural analysis of homelessness in general.

Though this book seeks to draw parallels and comparisons between Orwell's day and the present (and to that end we have included excerpts from Orwell's *Down and Out in Paris and London*), we have not followed his plan literally. Thus, although we investigated the life and conditions of work of present-day Paris *plongeurs* (and, basically, *plus ça change*), we chose instead to give an account of some of the French capital's floating population of homeless youth. They are, we believe, more representative of today's experience. Similarly, the present writer has taken the liberty of not rigidly following the order of Orwell's text in the excerpts selected. Instead, he hopes to have followed his spirit.

This book could not have been made without the help of many people: the large number of homeless people with whom we spent many hours and days, and the workers in voluntary agencies who answered our questions with unfailing generosity. In particular we would like to thank Rab MacWilliam, our editor at Penguin, Neil McIntosh of Shelter, Martin Jones of Piccadilly Advice Centre, Sarah Smith and David Moore in London, and Susan Croft and May in Paris. Much of the background material for Paris was culled from Theodore Zeldin's books on the French and their history. Thanks also to Grove Hardy for photographic printing and to Derek Bayes for photographic advice.

Sandy Craig
Chris Schwarz

# Paris

My hotel was called the Hôtel des Trois Moineaux. It was a dark, rickety warren of five storeys, cut up by wooden partitions into forty rooms. The rooms were small and inveterately dirty, for there was no maid, and Madame F., the *patronne*, had no time to do any sweeping. The walls were as thin as matchwood, and to hide the cracks they had been covered with layer after layer of pink paper, which had come loose and housed innumerable bugs. Near the ceiling long lines of bugs marched all day like columns of soldiers, and at night came down ravenously hungry, so that one had to get up every few hours and kill them in hecatombs . . .

The lodgers were a floating population, largely foreigners, who used to turn up without luggage, stay a week and then disappear again. They were of every trade – cobblers, bricklayers, stonemasons, navvies, students, prostitutes, rag-pickers. Some of them were fantastically poor . . .

There were eccentric characters in the hotel. The Paris slums are a gathering-place for eccentric people – people who have fallen into solitary, half-mad grooves of life and given up trying to be normal or decent. Poverty frees them from ordinary standards of behaviour, just as money frees people from work. Some of the lodgers in our hotel lived lives that were curious beyond words.

There were the Rougiers, for instance, an old, ragged, dwarfish couple who plied an extraordinary trade. They used to sell postcards on the Boulevard St Michel. The curious thing was that the postcards were sold in sealed packets as pornographic ones, but were actually photographs of chateaux on the Loire; the buyers did not discover this till too late, and of course never complained. The Rougiers earned about a hundred francs a week, and by strict economy managed to be always half starved and half drunk. The filth of their room was such that one could smell it on the floor below. According to Madame F., neither of the Rougiers had taken off their clothes for four years.

Central Paris bustles with commerce, shops, markets, with marionette traffic police and coveys of art sightseers and tourists, with demonstrating students and the solid bourgeois walking their dogs. With the motorists in their traffic jams. Alongside these, in greater numbers than you would expect, are the poor, sometimes indistinguishable in the crowd, sometimes obvious and shocking.

The poor: beggars, *clochards*, bums, panhandlers, punks, pickpockets, *zonards*, ex-convicts, street musicians and performers of all kinds, bohemians, Africans festooned with folksy leather handbags, sellers of dog-eared postcards, hippies, students handing out throwaway leaflets, gipsy kids with darting fingers, gipsy mothers with babies beseeching alms.

Like everybody in republican France the poor have the freedom of the streets. *Liberté, égalité, fraternité.* The streets are public property and therefore for the use of everyone. But principles stretch only so far. The poor have the freedom of the streets, but they have to watch out for the *Brigade Assistance aux Personnes Sans Accommodation*, or *les bleus* as they're known. *Les bleus* are police. They pick up the old *clochards*, the traditional picturesque Parisian street-tramps, and the younger travellers, or bums, as some of this international crew prefer to be called. Sometimes, even, *les bleus* catch a punk or a *zonard*, one of the homeless unemployed French youth. They pick them up and take them to the 'prison for the hungry' at Nanterre, a suburb of Paris.

For thirty years since the Second World War, the developed world, including Western Europe, has enjoyed an unparalleled period of prosperity. It is a prosperity achieved partly through the systematic underdevelopment of the non-industrial world, through neo-colonialism, the guest-worker system and other devices, partly through the harnessing of science and technology. By the early seventies it seemed as though poverty in the developed world might soon be finally vanquished. Plenty rather than scarcity was the norm.

Before this, the history of mankind had been the history of survival. Each generation was brought up in a world where scarcity was the norm. In this world, poverty, hunger and lack of shelter were not exceptional. Mankind developed many responses to combat this. In comparatively recent historical times, for instance, the family in all its extensions, the local community, the solidarity of fellow workers stood between the individual and absolute scarcity. The shopkeeper gave food on tick.

For perhaps the first time in history a generation has been brought up in a society where plenty is the norm. Meanwhile, scarcity for many of the antecedent generation is associated with war, which, in turn, is assumed to be an abnormal situation. During this period the younger generation have been trained how to live in a world of bounty. They have grown up with a set of expectations which, both in terms of the goods they would consume and the work at which they would be employed, were high.

Poverty, of course, remained, even if its rule had been substantially diminished. But it was thrust to the periphery. It was as though the occasional figure of the *clochard* – reckoned at 20,000 before the war, but only some 2,000 by the early seventies – was an exhibit in a museum, caught up in a time-warp. In the eighties, poverty has made a comeback.

Though they share the same pavements with them, the French speak of these people – the *zonards*, bums, *clochards* and those others scraping a perilous existence from odd casual jobs – as 'marginalized'. Typically, though, the term is used with specific reference to the young, those still in the process of being marginalized. Usually, these young are characterized as a generation brought up largely without skills or qualifications, without jobs and without much hope or desire for jobs, family life or anything remotely resembling the pattern of living adopted by their parents' generation. They are the disaffected youth, what *Newsweek* calls 'the lost generation'.

Perhaps it is more accurate to place the emphasis, as the French do, on those processes which seek to exclude these young people from the mainstream of life. Perhaps they are not so much 'the lost generation' as the cast-out generation.

Most people believe that they play no part in this process of marginalization. The *zonards* and the *clochards* in France – and the dossers in England – are down-and-outs either because they choose that lifestyle or because they have fallen prey to large-scale economic forces. Both of these beliefs contain a grain of truth. Both also neglect the major part of the truth: we all assist, if only in minor ways, in the process of marginalization.

The First of May Demonstration. Banners, placards, chants, leaflets, barrages of distorted sound from loudspeakers on top of vans, a mood of festivity in which everyone shares. Every left-wing group appears to be there: trade unions from both the main union organizations (the first time for some years), communists, anarchists, feminists, Solidarity supporters, anti-Khomeini demonstrators, militant émigré groups, the Legalize Cannabis lobby.

The *zonards* – mainly punks and *babacools*, the young new-style hippies – are grouped under the Legalize Cannabis banner, but after half an hour, too excited and too undisciplined to wait patiently, they take off down the pavement. Two hundred metres down the route the main march begins slowly to creak forward. There is a din of communist slogans in favour of banning foreign imports. Suddenly, a gap appears in the march. The *zonards* make for it. But immediately, communist stewards link arms and plug the gap. At the Place de la République the stewards seize the tactical advantage and block the pavement.

They divert the *zonards*. They make certain that they have no place in this great march of solidarity. By forcing them down a sidestreet, they marginalize the *zonards*. Should the *zonards* continue marching down the sidestreet (as they do, almost overturning a Renault 4 van in their frustration), they will make contact with the CRS, the riot police, who are monitoring the march from a distance of a few hundred metres. There the job of marginalization will be completed (and is: the *zonards* are dispersed).

---

It is altogether curious, your first contact with poverty. You have thought so much about poverty – it is the thing you have feared all your life, the thing you knew would happen to you sooner or later; and it is all so utterly and prosaically different. You thought it would be quite simple; it is extraordinarily complicated. You thought it would be terrible; it is merely squalid and boring. It is the peculiar *lowness* of poverty that you discover first; the shifts that it puts you to, the complicated meanness, the crust-wiping . . .

You discover the extreme precariousness of your six francs a day. Many disasters happen and rob you of food. You have spent your last eighty centimes on half a litre of milk, and are boiling it over the spirit lamp. While it boils a bug runs down your forearm; you give the bug a flick with your nail, and it falls, plop! straight into the milk. There is nothing for it but to throw the milk away and go foodless . . .

You go to the greengrocer's to spend a franc on a kilogram of potatoes. But one of the pieces that make up the franc is a Belgian piece, and the shopman refuses it. You slink out of the shop, and can never go there again . . .

You discover what it is like to be hungry. With bread and margarine in your belly, you go out and look into the shop windows. Everywhere there is food insulting you in huge, wasteful piles; whole dead pigs, baskets of hot loaves, great yellow blocks of butter, strings of sausages, mountains of potatoes, vast Gruyère cheeses like grindstones. A snivelling self-pity comes over you at the sight of so much food. You plan to grab a loaf and run, swallowing it before they catch you; and you refrain, from pure funk.

You discover the boredom which is inseparable from poverty; the times when you have nothing to do and, being underfed, can interest yourself in nothing. For half a day at a time you lie on your bed, feeling like the *jeune squelette* in Baudelaire's poem. Only food could rouse you. You discover that a man who has gone even a week on bread and margarine is not a man any longer, only a belly with a few accessory organs.

This – one could describe it further, but it is all in the same style – is life on six francs a day. Thousands of people in Paris live it – struggling artists and students, prostitutes when their luck is out, out-of-work people of all kinds. It is the suburbs, as it were, of poverty.

I continued in this style for about three weeks . . . These three weeks were squalid and uncomfortable, and evidently there was worse coming, for my rent would be due before long. Nevertheless, things were not a quarter as bad as I had expected. For, when you are approaching poverty, you make one discovery which outweighs some of the others. You discover boredom and mean complications and the beginnings of hunger, but you also discover the great redeeming feature of poverty: the fact that it annihilates the future. Within certain limits, it is actually true that the less money you have, the less you worry. When you have a hundred francs in the world you are liable to the most craven panics. When you have only three francs you are quite indifferent; for three francs will feed you till tomorrow, and you cannot think further than that. You are bored, but you are not afraid. You think vaguely, 'I shall be starving in a day or two – shocking isn't it?' And then the mind wanders to other topics. A bread and margarine diet does, to some extent, provide its own anodyne.

And there is another feeling that is a great consolation in poverty. I believe everyone who has been hard up has experienced it. It is a feeling of relief, almost of pleasure, at knowing yourself at last genuinely down and out. You have talked so often of going to the dogs – and well, here are the dogs, and you have reached them, and you can stand it. It takes off a lot of anxiety.

---

All day trouble has been cooking down here in the close, dusty, clanging air at the bottom of the Forum des Halles. Even the concourse cleaner with his orange overalls and his snap-can at the end of a stick is acting up bilious. The thunderous atmosphere has made everyone thick in the head. So it's no surprise that the afternoon ends with a fight.

The Forum des Halles. They have completely stripped away the old market. Not even the memory of a rotting vegetable remains: such a thought would be heretical. In its place they are building a glittering antiseptic construction of one-way glass, steel, gracefully curved aluminium and snow-white concrete. There are tiered arcades of splendid, useless boutiques and expensive indoor pavement cafés. Outside, upstairs, behind the sheer cliffs of one-way glass, are studios in which choirs of budding musicians can dimly be seen practising.

There is a central sunken forum which can be reached from the bottom level of the shopping piazza, up a short flight of granite steps. The *zonards* hang out on the steps. This is where the fight takes place.

All afternoon a group of older rockers in leather jackets and jeans have been laying down the law, trying to ban glue from the steps. Their leader, Georges, argues aggressively, with much waving of his arms. Glue bags are confiscated from the punks. When the offenders persist, violence is the only answer.

When the fight happens it is almost gladiatoral. The rockers choose one of their lieutenants, a wiry *bandito* who struts like a prize fighting cock. His adversary is a punk with SID tattooed on his shaven temple and eyes glazed from glue.

The fight itself lasts only a few minutes. It is punctuated by breaks which, though they last only a few seconds, are like the intervals between acts at the theatre: they heighten the spectacle. From the first blow it is obvious that the prize cock will win. Only one thing almost prevents this foregone conclusion when, while they wrestle on the ground at the foot of the steps, two *flics* walk by. But the police, though they spot the fight, continue past the crowded *zonards* and up the escalator. The prize cock nuts Sid twice.

Then, somehow and against the odds, Sid is up on his feet, shuffling, making a show at boxing. It is graceful, old-fashioned, bound to fail. The prize cock starts battering him. A few seconds later Sid offers his hand. It is a gesture which tries to maintain the pretence that it was all a bit of a lark. He is trying to finish the fight without admitting that he has been defeated. The prize cock seems to agree, then hits him again. Sid sits down sullenly on the steps. The prize cock hits him hard on the cheek. It is half-punch, half-slap. He is shaming Sid now. He is also conscious of the attention of the crowd. He is enjoying both his physical power over Sid and its theatrical extension – his power over the crowd.

After Sid's defeat, the rockers move in on the other punks and strip them of their badges, collars, mementoes, swastikas, studs, chains, safety-pins. It is confiscation time. Afterwards, the punks shamble off in threes and fours, miserable, dejected. They go up the direct escalator to street level and wander off to the fountain.

A few minutes later, the police arrive in force. Quickly the steps are cleared and the concourse cleaner and his mate are enthusiastically slopping water over the steps.

This is one of the ways in which the authorities control the *zonards*. They wash the steps on which the *zonards* sit, forcing them outside. Nowhere else inside Les Halles gets washed so regularly or with so much determination and water. There is another method of control which is used later in the evening, after the boutiques and cafés have closed and the arcades and aisles are deserted. When the only people left are the *zonards* in the belly of Les Halles. That's the time when the police stroll along the upper balconies with their aerosol cans of tear gas, fingers on the buttons. A fine veil descends, invisible. It's nothing serious, but suddenly cigarettes taste sharp and nasty. People begin coughing and sneezing. Eyes begin to water.

The *zonards* come to the metropolis from every region of the country, from Corsica and Brittany, Luxembourg and the Midi and even further afield, and from the suburbs of Paris and Paris itself. Perhaps, originally, they came to look for work. Now they no longer even make a show of looking for work.

They are not unintelligent. They know that any job they were offered would be hard, disagreeable, without status. It would lead nowhere. Worse, they know that any job they were offered would not be well-paid and that the money they earned from that job would be insufficient to purchase the commodities that the whole impetus of the media and their education has taught them to see as valuable. They just wouldn't have enough money to buy all those things which society says make life worth living. They know all this because some of them have had those kinds of jobs and have chucked them in to come to Paris. And because, anyway, it's obvious. Obvious to anyone with half a brain, though sometimes the parents kick up a fuss. So they drift. And gravitate, perhaps, to Les Halles.

Not all do. A lot remain in the suburbs of Paris, some go south to Cannes and the Riviera. Different gangs hang out in different parts – rockers in Montparnasse, a breed of punks on mopeds in Bourg-la-Reine. And though you get some rastas up on the second tier of arcades at Les Halles, mostly the Africans and North Africans and Arabs stay in their quarters, around Barbès and Belleville, where drugs are easier to come by, heroin as well as hash. Decaying, half-demolished ghettos that the *zonards* of Les Halles visit only now and then, only if there is a reason.

––––––––––

It was midday before Boris decided to get up. All the clothes he now had left were one suit, with one shirt, collar and tie, a pair of shoes almost worn out, and a pair of socks all holes. He had also an overcoat which was to be pawned in the last extremity. He had a suitcase, a wretched twenty-franc cardboard thing, but very important, because the *patron* of the hotel believed that it was full of clothes – without that, he would probably have turned Boris out of doors. What it actually contained were the medals and photographs, various odds and ends, and huge bundles of love-letters. In spite of all this Boris managed to keep a fairly smart appearance. He shaved without soap and with a razor-blade two months old, tied his tie so that the holes did not show, and carefully stuffed the soles of his shoes with newspaper. Finally, when he was dressed, he produced an ink-bottle and inked the skin of his ankles where it showed through his socks. You would never have thought, when it was finished, that he had recently been sleeping under the Seine bridges.

We went to a small café off the rue de Rivoli, a well-known rendezvous of hotel managers and employees. At the back was a dark, cave-like room where all kinds of hotel workers were sitting – smart young waiters, others not so smart and clearly hungry, fat pink cooks, greasy dishwashers, battered old scrubbing-women. Everyone had an untouched glass of black coffee in front of him. The place was, in effect, an employment bureau, and the money spent on drinks was the *patron's* commission. Sometimes a stout, important-looking man, obviously a restaurateur, would come in and speak to the barman, and the barman would call to one of the people at the back of the café. But he never called to Boris or me, and we left after two hours, as the etiquette was that you could only stay two hours for one drink. We learned afterwards, when it was too late, that the dodge was to bribe the barman; if you could afford twenty francs he would generally get you a job.

––––––––––

The shelves of the grocery shop off the rue de Seine are stacked with cans and packets. Even after two years in France he does not understand the writing on the labels but, through previous trial and error and careful study of the pictures on the packaging, he knows what is inside some of the cans.

Expertly he slips a can of *cassoulet* into the inner pocket of his jacket. Expertly, but not quite expertly enough: the shopkeeper, who has been keeping half an eye on him, spots him. He watches intently. He waits until he sees the man palm a pre-packed Camembert. Once he is certain, he is furious. He rushes across.

Afterwards, Tam bursts out laughing. 'It's a crease,' he says in his broad Glaswegian accent. 'They're headcases. It's often like that. They nab you and give you a right bollocking and you think, "Shite, this is me for the high jump, it's the polis this time." And then they boot you out the door ...'

Davy, Tam's mate and also from Cambuslang, breaks in. 'Aye, but the bit that gets me is when they let you keep the stuff you've thieved. I mean, that's plain saft.'

'Right enough. But they remember you fine. You cannae walk in that door again. You're barred for life.'

Tam and Davy are in their late twenties, have been on the road for three years. They are, in their own words, 'professional bums', living by begging, shoplifting and scavenging. They still cannot quite believe how easy it all is in Paris.

Unlike in London, where the corner shop has been squeezed out by big business, property speculators and the chain stores, the heart of Paris is crowded with small shops of every kind. There are various reasons for this. The lack of credit, at least until recently, hampered the usual trend in developing countries towards larger groupings and monopolization. Laws and taxes penalized larger shops and supported the smaller family business. Perhaps more importantly, the ideal of the shopkeeper – who wages a continuous guerilla war against the State and conceals the majority of his takings from the taxman – is to make enough money quickly in order to be able to retire early to live off his capital. For this reason, since prices and profit margins are kept high, he can, financially, tolerate a certain level of petty pilfering. And, maybe, he has a little sympathy for the shoplifter; maybe he just doesn't want to get entangled with the bureaucracy of police and courts.

Joie, one of the *zonards* from Les Halles, is sitting in front of a half-finished *crème* in O'Kitch, the McDonalds of Paris. This branch is situated between Les Halles and the Pompidou Centre, a cobbled pedestrian area thronging with crowds. Inside O'Kitch, the video loop shows Dexy's Midnight Runners singing 'Come On Eileen', the hit song of the moment in Paris. They are dressed like scrawny nineteenth-century Irish peasants, like poor white trash.

Outside, Marc and Judes are panhandling – *faire la manche*, showing the sleeve, as it's called. Occasionally, Judes's narrow intelligent face looks furtive. More often though, and particularly when panhandling, it looks trustworthy. He could be a good panhandler, but isn't. He can't be bothered working at it. Neither can Marc. He has coarse good looks and enjoys life. That's about all that can be said about Marc: he's the kind of person who doesn't leave much of an impression. Most of the time he's listening to Pink Floyd on his Sony Walkman. He is the definitive *babacool* – into sixties hippy fashion, into peace and love (after a fashion), but mostly into laziness.

Usually Marcel works with them. He panhandles in an off-hand way. He doesn't care if anyone gives him money or not. If they don't give him money, so what? It's no big cheese. And if they're smoking a cigarette, he'll try again for a smoke. Maybe he can embarrass them a little. Sometimes, if he's in a bad mood or just feeling crazy (something which happens not infrequently), he'll send up the tourists, particularly those who refuse to give. If you're a tourist, his philosophy goes, then you're fair game, you've got to have money. And if you don't give, then you're just plain mean – and the mean have to be sent up. It's almost a duty. So he sends them up. He's a good mimic and a natural clown, but he's pretty lousy when it comes to *faire la manche*. Still, no one minds: you've got to have a few jokes to break the tedium of panhandling, the boredom of everything … But today, Marcel is off somewhere, making a last desperate legal attempt to avoid National Service.

'Begging,' says Judes, 'is work. It's as simple and awful as that.' It occupies time, it takes up energy, it's a drag. Just as on the production line, it involves the same thing over and over again, the same sequence of physical movements, gestures, words. Who wants to work on the production line? Who wants to panhandle for long?

Joie acts as banker. When they've collected a little money they take it to her. Then they return to beg. The reason Joie doesn't panhandle is that she is under eighteen and looks it. Until she reaches her majority the police can pick her up and return her to her parents. Joie has spent much of the last two or three years running away from home, truanting from school. She doesn't want to be hauled back to her parents; they're all right, but this is the life for her. She can hardly wait until she is eighteen, then she'll travel the world.

Joie is Vietnamese. Fifteen years ago her father, who was a member of the Vietnamese middle class, managed to find a job in Paris. After three years he had saved enough money to bring his wife and only daughter out. They escaped from Vietnam shortly before the fall of Saigon. Joie has only a few memories of that time before her life in Paris – her nextdoor neighbours, her kindergarten, bombs falling. I imagine dappled sunlight falling across a quiet backstreet in a prosperous quarter of Saigon. Far away in the distance, rice fields. Then, almost immediately, I imagine the skies darkening, police and soldiers searching motorcyclists in the street …

Her parents cannot understand why she will not accept the education and the chance of a better life that they are offering her. They have brought her halfway across the world to safety and now she courts disaster. She associates with youths they do not like, youths who are plainly unsuitable.

Joie and Judes are in love, first love. 'We've been together five months,' she says happily, then teases, 'for me, it's a record.' Judes gets serious at this and tells her off: in this life one doesn't provoke the gods. He and Marc have finished their *crème* (Marcel only drinks his coffee black) and slope off to do another few minutes' panhandling, smoking their Marlboros.

Sometimes Joie's parents' guard slips and they become acutely conscious of their own displacement. They have been forced to abandon one life and with it the landscape, both social and geographic, that surrounded it and helped make sense of it. Landscapes are like languages in that they can make sense of life but, unlike languages, they are tied to one place. The meanings of that place, both the physical and social geography of it, cannot be adequately translated to another location. Instead the other place must impose its own meanings.

Each of us has a precise sense of locality. For some it is acute; for others it is no more than the occasional nagging sense of unease. There is one place, one landscape we recognize as home.

In moments like these, Joie's parents think that her destiny was formed from the instant of her birth. They prefer to believe this rather than contemplate the alternative – that Joie chose to become a *zonard*.

It is, anyway, more complicated than a simple matter of choice: how heavily were the scales weighted to begin with?

Mostly they survey the situation with what in Western terms would be called stoical pragmatism. They have no tradition of youth rebellion yet they understand that the passage between childhood and majority is frequently difficult.

After a time, usually just a few minutes, panhandling gets indescribably tedious. Judes's face grows more and more lugubrious. Marc has turned the volume up on his Walkman. 'You can't keep this up for long,' Judes says, grimacing and shaking his head. 'You have to have a break ...' He had a job once in his hometown before his motorcycle accident. At least with panhandling you can take a break when you want. He shrugs when he thinks of his hometown, his job, his parents. He doesn't think badly of them, truth to tell he hardly thinks of them at all these days.

He calls over to Marc, who has turned the volume up so much on his Walkman that he is beginning to shout instead of beg. 'You have to drown out reality sometimes,' Marc confides later. In the meantime, they give up panhandling. A few minutes of that, then a few minutes at O'Kitch, then a few minutes down the steps or maybe over at the fountain. No point in thinking about the past, no point in thinking too hard about the future either ...

Davy sits cross-legged, head slumped forward, against the wall of the metro corridor at the Odéon. He holds a cardboard square in front of his face which reads: 'Please would you have two or three francs for eating. Thank you.' The writing is crude, childish. Only the top of Davy's curly head is visible.

Tam keeps fifty metres' distance, on the lookout. 'The blues spotted us once,' he explains. 'We didnae see them until they were on top of us. We had to do a flier. So now one of us begs and the other yin keeps his eyes peeled. It's safer that way.'

Half an hour passes. Few people put anything into Davy's blackened tartan bonnet. Time seems to lengthen out, to become interminable. There's a digital clock near by which Tam keeps glancing at. 'You try and last an hour if you can. It fair gets to you, real head-banging stuff. Don't let anyone ever tell you begging isn't hard work. And it gets harder all the time. Maybe wees should form a union,' he jokes. 'I mean, there's enough of us doing it now. Just pause to consider it for a wee moment. You're out there in all kinds of weather, you've got nae holidays to look forward to, no sick pay, nothing . . .'

He lapses into silence, takes another look at the clock. He doesn't mention the lack of a pension. Perhaps he doesn't think about it.

A quarter of an hour later a little boy no more than seven pauses in front of Davy and regards him gravely. He has a satchel strapped across his back. His face is as polished as his shoes. Eventually he makes up his mind, digs his hand into his pocket, and places his few centimes into Davy's bonnet.

'Aw Jesus,' mutters Tam. 'Will you look at that? I tell you it's a fair choker, this job. Sometimes you'll get some old granny doddering over and dropping you fifty centimes out of her purse. It turns you over inside. See, that's why we stop when we've got enough. Survival, plus maybe ten francs clear. Otherwise we'd be exploiting the punters and that wouldn't be right. It's hard enough on the head as it is. Mind, you can net a fair whack if you work at it. A hundred francs a day, hundred and fifty maybe if Lady Luck is smiling.'

Their average day. Up at around midday from their sleeping pitch under Pont Neuf and along to the student cafeteria at the Sorbonne for lunch. 'You've got to look after yourself in this life. You'd just sink without one hot meal inside your belly every day.' After lunch, the afternoon – or as much of it as they can stand – is spent begging. And then, in the evening, they go on the wine. Later, when they feel it's safe and *les bleus* have gone, they return to their pitch below Pont Neuf.

The hour is almost through. Tam is gearing himself up for his stint. An immaculately groomed lady trailing a Pekinese elegantly behind her strolls past Davy on her high heels, then stops and returns. She begins talking to Davy. Tam groans. 'Another mad fucker. I tell you, begging attracts them like fleas. Because youse are on the streets they think you're easy meat.'

The lady is telling Davy that if he comes with her she will buy him a burger. Her dog is sniffing Davy's bonnet suspiciously. Davy swears back in English. Unperturbed the lady switches to English. 'Aw listen,' says Davy, 'have a fucking heart. Just give us a franc or two.'

'No, I wish to buy you a burger.'

Tam signals to Davy to go ahead. 'Okey-dokey then. A burger it is.'

The woman pauses. 'The problem is I don't believe there's a restaurant in the direction I'm walking.'

'Well then, one of them Tunisian sandwiches will suit me fine. They're grand.'

'No, I was meaning to buy you a burger. That's what I wanted to give you.'

'All right then,' Tam says, exasperated, 'if youse gives me the money, I'll take myself off and find a burger bar.' She hands over a franc. 'Here, I can't buy the fucking bun to wrap round the burger with this!'

'No. But if I gave you the money, could I be certain that you'd spend it on a burger? I don't honestly think I could, you know. I think you'd just squander it on wine.'

'Naw, not me,' Davy replies drily. 'I'd put it in my piggy-bank. Me and my pal are saving up for a ghetto-blaster.'

Tam shakes his head wearily. 'Half the time, I reckon, they don't even realize themselves that they're getting a kick out of youse.' He watched her languidly departing. 'People like that need people like us to keep them feeling superior.'

---

It was the first time that I had been in a French pawnshop. One went through grandiose stone portals (marked, of course, 'Liberté, Égalité, Fraternité' – they write that even over the police stations in France) into a large, bare room like a school classroom, with a counter and rows of benches. Forty or fifty people were waiting. One handed one's pledge over the counter and sat down. Presently, when the clerk had assessed its value he would call out, 'Numéro such and such, will you take fifty francs?' Sometimes it was only fifteen francs, or ten, or five – whatever it was, the whole room knew it. As I came in the clerk called with an air of offence, 'Numéro 83 – here!' and gave a little whistle and a beckon, as though calling a dog. Numéro 83 stepped to the counter; he was an old bearded man, with an overcoat buttoned up at the neck and frayed trouser-ends. Without a word the clerk shot the bundle across the counter – evidently it was worth nothing. It fell to the ground and came open, displaying four pairs of men's woollen pants. No one could help laughing. Poor Numéro 83 gathered up his pants and shambled out, muttering to himself.

---

Jacques and Francine are always moaning. Were they born some thirty or thirty-five years ago moaning, or is it only since they met each other that they've fallen into the habit? Who knows? Today, they dig their arms into their shapeless clothes, look at the Seine and grumble.

This spring the Seine has flooded its banks. For weeks it has been impossible to sleep out under the bridges. Jacques and Francine regard the rain and the rising of the Seine almost as a personal insult. Jacques, disgusted, looks up at the clouds. Francine brings out one of her English expressions. 'That's life,' she says archly. She has a small collection of much-loved English expressions. When she utters them, it is as though she is displaying them, as though they are trophies.

"Rain is particularly bad for business,' Jacques declares. 'People don't want to give when it's raining. Or perhaps they do, but they're in too much of a rush.' Jacques and Francine beg together, huddled up, hunched into the angle of a wall, holding the usual small cardboard notice. They wear hang-dog expressions and look altogether a pitiable sight. But she takes offence if their begging is considered a sham. She shows her bad ankle, swollen and discoloured. And she makes Jacques, already grumbling that the posture makes his back sore and that when he is old he is sure to have a stoop, roll up his trouser leg to display a leprous nine-inch scar running across his calf. Francine produces another English expression from her treasure trove. 'It's terrible, my dears, simply terrible.'

For them, begging is work. Lousy work, to be sure. But they don't feel the shame and humiliation that Tam and Davy do, or at least not to the same sharp degree. Perhaps because, having been brought up in France, a Catholic country with a Catholic tradition of alms-giving, they see begging as 'normal'. Whereas for Tam and Davy, with the Protestant work ethic on their backs, begging is abnormal and shameful.

Jacques tells the story, with interjections from Francine, of the last time they were picked up by *les bleus*. 'We were living in a small hotel in Montmartre, seventy-eight francs per night for both of us, including break- fast. Good, eh? –' ('It was the tops,' interjects Francine.) 'But, of course, it meant that we had to work much longer hours, from nine in the morning until eight at night. To pay for the room –' ('Terrible, my dears, but that's life!') 'And then, one day, *les bleus* picked us up. Well, I argued with them. I told them we weren't out on the streets. That we lived in a hotel. I even had a hundred francs in my pocket. They're not supposed to pick you up if you've got more than five francs, but it didn't do any good. The bastards!' (Francine's English proves inadequate. She resorts to a string of French oaths.) 'Nanterre, the prison for the hungry. God, that place stinks. You get all sorts there – drunkards, alcoholics, bums, madmen.'

Ziggy, a German wayfarer who has been staying in Paris for some weeks, hobbles down from the *quai* and trades Jacques a disposable razor for a German newspaper Jacques found in a bin. Immediately he starts scanning the crime pages, while Jacques, suddenly animated, creakily stands up. 'I really fancy a shave. It's so much nicer. Ugh, you've no idea how I hate these bristles. I'm not a *clochard* yet, you know. Not by a long chalk. Come on, *ma petite*,' he says gently to Francine, helping her up. 'Let's go to work.' He turns and explains: 'It costs one franc twenty centimes for hot water at the local wash-house. I wasn't going to bother working for a bit, but this is worth it. Of course, we won't stop there. We'll get enough for a bite to eat. Enough for a feast!'

From the moment they were picked up by *les bleus* they squabbled. There is always something slightly pathetic about two old men fighting, perhaps because the threat of physical force falls far short of the emotional venom of the argument. But with these two *clochards* with their flailing arms, the scene is even more ludicrous. It's as though their arms are trying to embrace the other as much as fight him, as though their friendship is built around squabbles like these. One argues and, to emphasize the point, takes a drink from their bottle of *vin ordinaire*, then passes the bottle to his mate.

'I told you they'd be coming round. I said we should move off. Now look what's happened . . .'

'How was I to know they'd change their routine? They never usually come this far out on Mondays. Hey, you – how come you're out here today? It is Monday, isn't it?'

The officer, a sergeant, nods. Behind him can be heard the continuous sound of the traffic on the Périphérique, Paris's motorway ring road. Clutching their few possessions, which they keep in plastic carrier bags, and still arguing fiercely, the two old *clochards* stumble towards the bus. Every day, except Sunday, *les bleus* tour Paris in a grey converted Paris bus. The bus is partitioned into two unequal halves. In the smaller front half sit the police. In the larger back half stand the *clochards* and other travellers picked up by the police. The doors to the back half can only be opened from the outside.

Some of the *clochards* are volunteers: these wait twice daily by Châtelet for the bus to turn up. But the majority do not wish to go. For these, *les bleus* use typical police tactics. When they see some *clochards* in a park, they emerge from the bus at a brisk trot and surround their prey, cutting off any possibility of escape with pincer movements.

Some of the *clochards* go quietly. Others protest, even though they know it will make no difference: once *les bleus* have decided to pick someone up, then there is no alternative. The decision has already been made; it's out of anyone's hands. Not that *les bleus*, despite their guns, use force: persuasion is all that is necessary.

They justify their job in various ways. The sergeant on the bus believes that there shouldn't be *clochards* in a socialist France, that Mitterrand should have done him out of a job. He is an upholder of liberty and it pains him personally when, as sometimes happens, they get stick from passers-by. They are, after all, only doing their job. And it is a necessary service: at Nanterre the *clochards* will be cleaned, given food, checked for TB. First aid will be administered and they will receive shelter for the night. In the morning they will be issued with a pass for the metro so that they can return to their quarter. In this way, the sergeant insists, his job is a service to humanity.

At the bus the two *clochards*, squabbling and swigging from their bottle, are bureaucratically processed: forms have to be filled in, precise records kept. The sergeant asks for their identity cards.

'Don't have an identity card,' one mutters. 'I don't see why anyone should have to have an identity card. Officialdom, that's all.'

'Interfering,' agrees the other, nodding vigorously. 'I thought this was supposed to be a free country.'

Patiently the sergeant rips up his Gitane packet. On the back of the label he takes down the *clochard*'s particulars: name, date of birth, place of birth. His handwriting is neat, schoolboyish. He hands this square of cardboard to the *clochard*; this for the moment at least will suffice as an identity card. The two friends are loaded into the back of the bus and the doors close behind them with a pneumatic hiss.

BAPSA - to give *les bleus* their official initials - are based in La Villette, an old working-class quarter which straddles the Canal St Denis. The whole quarter is covered in a fine dust from the warehouses and factories. Men sit in groups on the benches by the canal and fish with the attitude of those who never catch anything. It is as though the dust has settled over them.

The chief of *les bleus* recites his grim statistics, but without enthusiasm. It is as though they pain him personally. In 1979 his service recorded 4,219 *clochards* and travellers; in 1981 this number had risen to 6,372; in 1982 to 6,806. Of these latter, 6,339 were men and 467 women. 5,173 of them were French.

There are other clear trends. He is emphatic that some travellers - the term he uses for the younger bums - become *clochards*, though he worries what kind of *clochard* they will turn into. More and more, his service is taking comparative youngsters to Nanterre. He is disturbed by this; disturbed, too, by the violence of this younger generation.

He grows philosophical. Like most Parisians he likes the old *clochards* - harmless characters who kept themselves to themselves, who made a square, a park or a hot-air vent above the metro their home and were content so long as they were allowed to drink in peace. Picturesque, even perhaps a necessary antidote to the increasing rationalization of modern life. He speaks of them with affection. But he is perturbed by the younger people. They are often violent, often involved in mugging, pickpocketing, street crime, shoplifting. He doesn't understand why and he doesn't see any solution. Times are changing and so, too, is the behaviour of the homeless.

He thinks that at bottom it is the fault of society.

But does their behaviour not indicate something else? Is it not a distorted reflection of some of the cruder and more destructive values of the culture which affects us all? Are these 'bums' not perhaps caricatures of mainstream society? Can we not see their lifestyle as aping that of bourgeois society, which, in their terms, is both useless and uncaring?

These are not his thoughts; but he shares a similar sense of indictment of society. He does not say so in as many words, but perhaps he senses that as the nature and experience of homelessness changes, so society's response to it becomes inadequate and out of date.

In the bus, the two old friends fall to squabbling again. They even attempt one or two weak, frightened punches. The sergeant raps peremptorily on the glass partition, like a schoolmaster, and they stop; but at that moment the bus lurches and the bottle of wine falls. A few seconds later a trickle of wine oozes under the partition, bringing with it a faint sour whiff from the back of the bus. After a time it looks like dirty dried blood.

*

Compared with the age of the world, the history of mankind is ephemeral. Compared to the history of mankind, the history of childhood is fugitive and fleeting. The history of adolescence has only just begun. France was, perhaps, the first country in which the category of adolescence became apparent. By 1930, over one hundred novels had been published on the theme. It became a separate category between infancy and adulthood with its own problems and characteristics.

A cult of adolescence developed in protest against adult values. André Gide praised the adolescent qualities of restlessness, anxiety, desire, hatred for the family. Henry de Montherlant saw it as a new social malaise. Mauriac saw adolescents as an isolated group shut off from adults 'by a wall of timidity, shame, incomprehension and hurt feelings'. Many adults simply feared adolescents: a survey carried out in 1905 had shown that the number of minors accused of homicide, arson, assault, vagabondage, theft was almost double that of adults.

In the 1950s, a sample of French people were asked which commandment they considered the most important. The fifth, 'Honour your parents', won easily. Meanwhile, psychologists were characterizing the group behaviour of adolescents as: complete freedom of speech and expression, violent hatred of other cliques, slander of everything outside the group. The ties within the group were seen as akin to blood bondage, but friendship itself, although often paraded, was thought to be unreliable.

Thirty years later all these partial truths have become overlaid with the explosion in youth cultures and, latterly, the economic crisis of the West. Youth has taken on an international dimension. Beatniks, rockers, hell's angels, mods, hippies, skinheads, punks: the youth rebellions of the past thirty years have been rebellions against straight society and the adult world. Yet as each successive wave defined youth's identity, it was colonized, customized and co-opted by capitalism. Rebellion was marketed and transformed into style. For a quarter of a century the parasitical nature of this relationship has fostered the creative energy of these rebellions.

Once again the rebellion has changed its form. At first sight, the energy seems to have dissipated. It's as though youth rebellion is no longer creative, as though nowadays it merely parodies the rebellions of the past. But perhaps this is the final rebellion – a scavenging of past revolts, constantly changing its emphasis and its style so that the fashion and image industry can never catch up, never package their dissent.

There is one important difference between today's rebellion and those of the past. Then, the kids had money in their pockets, sometimes even money to burn. Many were working; the others could look forward to a future of work. There were plenty of opportunities. Those rebellions represented only a temporary rejection of society – soon, in a year, or two years, they would settle down, marry, have kids, be clothed in the comfortable lifestyle that came with the job. Meanwhile, they would consume the things that gave them their identity and cock a snook at the adult world. But now, nobody has anything. There are few jobs - and anyway jobs are a bore and hardly worth the trouble. Plus, the lifestyle that's still promised, but rarely delivered, isn't so comfortable, looks more precarious. Maybe this time, the rejection will be permanent. Maybe this time, it's for keeps . . .

What has the adult world got left, anyway, except fantasies? A white Morgan drives down the Champs-Élysées. Marcel looks up from the pavement painting being drawn by his hero, Alexandre. He is entranced. It is so cool. He points it out to the gang. It is flash, powerful, beautiful, the embodiment of a promise. But when the promise delivers a second-hand Renault 4? That's worse than a spit in the eye. All those Renault 4s. Who wants to live like that? It tires him out thinking about it. Better to drift.

As for the punks, theirs is a world where the authentic is always threatened with replacement by the kitch. The kitch is the adult world's way of controlling them, of substituting the brand name for the authentic experience.

The necessity to defend the authentic nature of their experience partly explains the endless discussions on the steps of Les Halles about punk. Sid and his mate sneer, wave their arms, indicating the other punks on the steps. 'They're punks of '83, not real punks. We're '77 punks. Punk is dead.' Georges, leader of the rockers, dismisses them all. 'These aren't real punks. They're peace punks, hippies in disguise. Real punks, now they were different. Real punks were violent, they didn't sniff glue.'

Up on the balcony overlooking the steps Michel, Pierre and Sebastien are sharing a bottle of sweet white wine. Sebastien, a one-handed scruff, belches. 'Punk is in the head,' he proclaims. 'Those punks down there. For them it's just a fashion.' He pushes his face close to mine. 'I don't like them,' he hisses. He unzips himself and pisses against the wall to the disgust of the passing window-shoppers. His action isn't a comment on what he has just said. Nor should it be interpreted as a protest against the world. It is part bravado, part natural bodily function. 'I am also gay,' he grins, waggling his engorged cock.

----

. . . Day after day Boris and I went up and down Paris, drifting at two miles an hour through the crowds, bored and hungry, and finding nothing. One day, I remember, we crossed the Seine eleven times. We loitered for hours outside service doorways, and when the manager came out we would go up to him ingratiatingly, cap in hand. We always got the same answer: they did not want a lame man, nor a man without experience. Once we were very nearly engaged. While we spoke to the manager Boris stood straight upright, not supporting himself with his stick, and the manager did not see that he was lame. 'Yes,' he said, 'we want two men in the cellars. Perhaps you would do. Come inside.' Then Boris moved, the game was up. 'Ah,' said the manager, 'you limp. *Malheureusement* –'

We enrolled our names at agencies and answered advertisements, but walking everywhere made us slow, and we seemed to miss every job by half an hour. Once we very nearly got a job swabbing out railway trucks, but at the last moment they rejected us in favour of Frenchmen. Once we answered an advertisement calling for hands at a circus. You had to shift benches and clean up litter, and, during the performance, stand on two tubs and let a lion jump through your legs. When we got to the place, an hour before the time named, we found a queue of fifty men already waiting. There is some attraction in lions, evidently.

---

History has known many migrations. However, it is only in the past 150 years since the Industrial Revolution that it has become saturated with them. Before, the most common forms of migration – nomadism and the seasonal migration of farmer following his stock from winter to summer pastures – served to preserve a rural society and a survival economy. The newer forms of migration have instead transformed rural societies into the urban, industrialized societies of the developed world. They have also underdeveloped large areas of the world from Africa to Corsica.

The most common form of recent migration is the emigration of poverty. There were three such emigrations in France during the nineteenth century, when hundreds of thousands of peasants, now marginal to rural society, were drawn to the local towns. There was a further emigration in 1936–8, involving some 330,000 people; but these instead were drawn to the larger, metropolitan cities, to Paris, Lyons, Marseilles. Increasingly, as capitalism has grown more wealthy, it has drawn its labour from a larger and larger hinterland. Since the Second World War this has included the Mediterranean basin and France's African colonies and ex-colonies. In each of these emigrations the peasants have been transformed into the sub-proletariat where the wages are lowest, the employment least secure and the labour least skilled.

But in addition to these emigrations of poverty there has also been a steady, continuous trickle from the country and regions of France to Paris and the other large centres. These people aren't the poorest. They are the young and the adventurous. In one study of Brittany in the 1950s it was found that 42 per cent of those who emigrated had made their decision to do so before the age of fourteen and another 35 per cent between the ages of fourteen and seventeen. This remains broadly true today. The zonards, for instance, aren't the most frustrated or least successful of the youth. Those with the least ability and imagination stay at home. So do the exceptionally talented or those with influential parents – they find work at home which satisfies them. It's the middle-ranking youth who are drawn to the metropolis.

The development of capitalism since the Second World War has created a new range of jobs – jobs in the media, in marketing, in education, in government, in finance, in the leisure and service industries. These white-collar jobs are not physically tiring and they are given a higher social status than unskilled labouring work.

As John Berger has stated, in *A Seventh Man*: 'This new category of work has altered the quality of remuneration expected for work in general. Remuneration now includes a lifestyle which, as it were, houses the wage even while being dependent on it.'

This was the status quo in the period of full employment which lasted until the mid seventies. A generation of future indigenous workers was brought up to expect that sort of work and that kind of lifestyle. With the recession of the past few years, they have been denied both. They will not now accept the old unskilled labouring work, not at any rate at the wages that are being offered. (And there is no likelihood that those wage rates will be dramatically increased.)

In order to preserve his integrity, the middle-ranking youth emigrates to the city and refuses to work in what he calls the 'shit' jobs. Between these and unemployment, he chooses unemployment. He chooses the lesser of two evils. He – and she, since though there are few women *clochards* there are many more women *zonards* – know that they will be accorded an inferior status and that this will be made apparent in a hundred ways: in the ready-made phrases, arguments and attitudes of the media (a media controlled by the adult world), by the institutions of society (the unemployment offices, the police, the banks – again, all controlled by the adult world), in the everyday etiquette of the city.

He and she acknowledge this fact by turning against this adult world, by antagonism. They withdraw into themselves and into their peer group, their own sub-culture. They reject the world as it rejects them. They mirror its reaction to them with their own reaction to it.

As well as the clans of punks, the *zonards* who hang around the bottom of Les Halles embrace many different cliques and characters. There is the rich girl from the suburbs who visits every Saturday and pretends she never has any cigarettes. There are Alain and his girlfriend Christine who sell homemade, rather ugly trinkets by the Pompidou Centre, mainly to Americans. Hélène, unsuccessfully studying photography. Louis, endlessly re-stringing and tuning his guitar on the steps, trying to overcome his inertia and get out and busk. (He played once, a beautiful slow country blues, tinged with melancholy.)

There is Émile. Émile is a *zonard* on Saturdays, and on weekday afternoons if he is on the night shift. He is an apprentice in a *boulangerie*. He has to do four years of that, then National Service, then he'll work in a *boulangerie* here in Paris until he's saved up enough money to buy his own business back in Brittany where he comes from. He reckons that'll take him ten years. Then, another ten or fifteen years in his own business. Then, as soon as possible, retirement and living off the proceeds. There is a dream in his eye, the dream of being a middle-aged *zonard*, of lazing around and smoking dope. Or whatever the equivalent is for a middle-aged *zonard*. For the moment he's lodging in a lousy hotel in the 20th arrondissement for 1,000 francs a month and learning his trade. And getting the hell out of there as often as he can, jumping the metro to Les Halles where he can drink and get doped up with his mates. He's a proficient musician, plays in a Breton folk-band; in fact, this evening they have a concert. But he smokes too much dope and drinks too much in the afternoon. In the end he can't be bothered turning up.

There is Suzanne. Suzanne is a summer and a holiday *zonard*. She is studying literature: Baudelaire, Rimbaud, as far back as Villon. 'Why do I come down here? I suppose it's because I like the people. My parents moved to Paris when I was fourteen. We lived in the 16th arrondissement, the posh quarter, just off Avenue Foch. For years I only knew the children of rich people, politicians, famous actresses. And then, one day, I suddenly discovered that there was another world. It excited me. I thought it was more real, more honest. Rich people don't know about poor people. They can't tell you a thing about them. They spend hours talking about them, but they get nowhere near the mark. Poor people know all about the rich. You can't escape it, they're in all the magazines and films. I've seen both sides. I know, despite what the media says, that the poor are just as interesting and worthwhile as the rich. I'll be back here this summer. And if there's nothing definite at university to return to, I'll probably end up staying on here. I don't know if the thought appeals or not. The French *zonard* is very lazy, you know. They always rely on others to get it together. They'll bum off anyone. They're always getting bored. Bored. But I like them. Maybe there's no other life for me.'

Then there are the groups who practise less legitimate trades. Judes and company, *babacools*, who survive by begging. Michel, Pierre and Sebastien who alternate begging with amateur pickpocketing. ('English girls are so stupid,' Michel announces one day, proudly displaying a purse with Barclaycard and passport. Sebastien empties it of money, then returns to where it was thieved; if he can find the owner, chances are that the reward will be greater than what they've found. 'They leave their handbags open for our fingers. It is the same only on a smaller scale,' he says, winding me up, 'as the Argentines and the shrimpish Falkland Islands.') And there's a number of ex-convicts with their secret symbols tattooed on the backs of their hands, and deserters from the Army.

Further down-market there's characters like Corse. Corse always acts crazy, is always sniffing glue, is always getting beaten up by the rockers. He is a punchie and going downhill fast. Goodness knows how he lives – he always speaks in impenetrable *zonard* slang, twisting words back to front, calling the punks 'kapons', the *flics* or *kepis*, as they're sometimes known, 'pikés'. ('Piquer' means to shoot up.)

And then there is Georges, leader of the rockers, whom we once see in a pimps' bar on the rue St Denis, the whores' hang-out. Georges is the overlord of the steps. He is an old-fashioned criminal apache. He delights in the preservation of order, *his* preservation of *his* order. It makes him feel strong. And that in turn, he says, makes him feel good. For Georges, Hitler was the only one who solved the *zonard/clochard* problem.

There are also one or two criminals; Philippe, for example, a professional pickpocket.

'Huh, I'm not like them. Look at this!' Philippe pulls out his rent receipt. His apartment – a one-room studio with the kitchen along one wall in the good part of Vincennes near the Bois – costs over 4,000 francs per month. This is more than the national minimum wage. 'I'm a professional pickpocket. For two months I went to school in M— and learned the trade. These days if I want I can make 1,000 francs a day. You can tell from people which pockets contain their valuables, they clutch them tightly. But, you see, in the metro there are always times when they have to open doors and then their pockets are unguarded. I've practised karate, *tai chi*. My fingers are light, supple but strong. And then I pass the pickings back to someone behind me. If people miss something, well, I've got nothing on me.

'Once I was picked up by the police but they couldn't nab me. I was working with my wife. She used to be a punk. We were walking arm in arm and she had her mirror out as though she was arranging her make-up. I stole a wallet. Then I looked in the mirror and saw two *flics* behind me. They had spotted me. So I quickly put the wallet back.

'My wife's expecting. We've had the tests. It's going to be a boy. I'd hoped for a girl but, well, it's a boy, a baby. I'm putting money into the bank for him, just in case something happens. There's 40,000 francs waiting for him in the bank. Once he's born I'm going to stop stealing. I'll find other work, legal. Then, I'll start talking to my neighbours, being the perfect bourgeois. They're mainly old and rich, leaning on sticks. They'd be horrified if they knew they had a pickpocket living in their block. I let sleeping dogs lie. I leave home every morning early, catch the metro, and I return every evening. They think I'm going off to the office like everybody else.'

---

My money oozed away – to eight francs, to four francs, to one franc, to twenty-five centimes – and twenty-five centimes is useless, for it will buy nothing except a newspaper. We went several days on dry bread, and then I was two and a half days with nothing to eat whatever. This was an ugly experience. There are people who do fasting cures of three weeks or more, and they say that fasting is quite pleasant after the fourth day; I do not know, never having gone beyond the third day. Probably it seems different when one is doing it voluntarily and is not underfed at the start.

The first day, too inert to look for work, I borrowed a rod and went fishing in the Seine, baiting with blue-bottles. I hoped to catch enough for a meal, but of course I did not. The Seine is full of dace, but they grew cunning during the siege of Paris, and none of them has been caught since, except in nets. On the second day I thought of pawning my overcoat, but it seemed too far to walk to the pawnshop, and I spent the day in bed, reading the *Memoirs of Sherlock Holmes*. It was all that I felt equal to, without food. Hunger reduces one to an utterly spineless, brainless condition, more like the after-effects of influenza than anything else. It is as though one had been turned into a jellyfish, or as though all one's blood had been pumped out and lukewarm water substituted. Complete inertia is my chief memory of hunger; that, and being obliged to spit very frequently, and the spittle being curiously white and flocculent, like cuckoo-spit. I do not know the reason for this, but everyone who has gone hungry several days has noticed it.

---

It is the last night at the Salvation Army's Emergency Night Hostel at La Villette. Tomorrow it is closing down to make way for a metro development. Perhaps because of this everyone is slightly on edge. Some are regulars here. For others it is their first night. Yet all participate, even if only slightly, in the communal sense of loss: tomorrow none of this will be here. The experience is distantly related to the experience of leaving home.

Anatole stands in front of his shaving-mirror slowly combing his black hair back in a sweep over his forehead. His eyes are concentrated on this task. He likes to keep himself looking good. This evening, for instance, he has already polished his shoes. In the *foyer*, as the hostel is called, he goes around in stockinged feet so that his shoes last longer. In the evening, as soon as he comes in, he hangs his expensive leather jacket on a clothes hanger. It was the last item of clothing he bought before he was made redundant from the small family business specializing in English sports and leisure wear and accessories – shooting sticks, deer-stalkers, rugby shirts, ribbed Shetland Wool socks and sleeveless jumpers.

That was some weeks ago. Despite his fastidious attention to his appearance, his attitude expresses resignation. Unlike the *zonards* and the *clochards* who – since they have, in the eyes of the French state, no activity – are ineligible for any social security payments, Anatole gets some unemployment benefit. But, all in all, it wasn't enough to pay the rent on his very expensive flat; so now he has ended up here. In the daytime he looks over the 'Situations Vacant' columns in the local papers, is always chasing after jobs. But already he feels defeated, deserted by his friends and, at thirty-five, as though he is over the hill.

Victor stumps into the dormitory, packages under his arm, building dust on his boots. He's been lucky again: it's the ninth day in a row he's found casual labouring work. His friend, a taciturn Algerian, follows him into the room.

'Hey, come on, Anatole,' he shouts in a throaty, cheerful voice. 'You look as though you've been swimming the wrong way up a sewer with your mouth open and swallowed a you-know-what. Shift your bum over here and grab a bite of real chow.'

Anatole goes over eagerly. Victor opens a paper parcel which contains some smoked fish. ('Fell off the back of a Hungarian meat lorry. Liberated it before those lousy farmers could picket it,' he laughs.) He flips open a bottle of *vin ordinaire*. The three of them eat and drink.

They've already eaten. The Salvation Army – which in France is a far cry from its parent body in England – provides them with a meal which, although basic and brought in, is adequate: vegetable soup, potatoes, steamed vegetables, bread. But, like any food which doesn't smack of charity, Victor's smoked fish tastes infinitely better.

The Salvation Army lodges upwards of 2,000 people a night in their Parisian hostels. Many of these come from the Ile de France, the area which surrounds Paris. The numbers are increasing rapidly; but their greatest concern is the large number of youngsters who are taking to the streets.

In a survey of the Emergency Night Shelter taken from 14 to 31 January 1983 – the French have a high regard for exact figures – the Salvation Army admitted 123 French males and 70 of foreign origin. These included small numbers of Algerians, English, Angolans, Belgians, Congolese, Egyptians, Ghanaians, Moroccans, Pakistanis, Rumanians, Vietnamese, Swiss, Tunisians, Turks and Zaïreans: from, in other words, more or less all over the world. The French males came from all over France and were aged between twenty and sixty, though the largest relative proportion were in their mid forties. Many of them were people on the borderline of work: just in work, just out of work or living by casual jobs.

Victor takes a drink of wine. 'I tell you what's the matter with this country. There's too many wogs, pure and simple. They come over here and take our jobs. I mean, you don't have to rub more than a couple of brain cells together to work it out for yourself. Even the CP are coming round to it. But as for the government, they're just shelling out to them left, right and centre. And we don't get a sniff of it.'

He hands the wine bottle to his Algerian mate. Racism, particularly against the Arabs and North Africans, is commonplace in Paris. The terrorist activities of ultra-right groups against Africans and, more particularly, against Jews has been well documented. Fascism is growing. Less well documented is the large-scale institutional racism. That the far right has not achieved significantly more penetration, given the simplicity of their arguments and the economic recession, is surprising. But at the moment the fascism of the bourgeoisie, of the small shopkeepers, of the law students, moves in a different world to that of the poor, the unemployed, the sub-proletariat.

Victor belches magnanimously. 'Come on, Anatole, look on the bright side! Every cloud has a silver lining. I was talking to the gaffer who's going to demolish this little lot, starting tomorrow. There's work going. I know it's not your line of country but I'm right in with him. We're like that –' (he crosses his fingers) – 'Soul-mates. Blood brothers. I could probably fix you up with something light.'

Anatole doesn't answer.

'God, sometimes you make me sick. You're wallowing in it. Don't you see that anything is better than nothing?'

The sergeant unlocks the massive steel doors set into a stone wall twelve feet high and the grey city bus of *les bleus* enters the 'prison for the hungry' at Nanterre. It is a bizarre, seemingly interminable institution – part modernized prison, part unmodernized, part hospital (of which part is open to the public), part workhouse, part old people's home. There are dormitories, cells, stone barracks.

Forty-nine people are unloaded from the bus and taken by the police inside. There, each *clochard* places all his possessions in a yellow plastic box: old newspapers, piles of letters, a few small coins, a comb, a handkerchief, a penknife, a plastic carrier bag. The police list these. Then the *clochard* signs and moves on. At this point he crosses an invisible line. He passes from police custody into the hospital service.

The *clochard* walks into the first section of the shower room. Here he strips and his clothes are taken from him. They will be disinfected and washed overnight. Then – although he is only vaguely supervised he knows it is impossible to escape this fate – he showers. The water contains disinfectant.

The scene in this first section of the shower room is indescribably foul. The smell is overpowering. Many haven't washed for weeks; one *clochard* has shit caked halfway up his back and down his legs. Many have sores, wounds and abrasions, some septic. Some have ulcerated legs and bad feet. There is a wheezing racket of coughing and spitting.

After showering they are dressed in greyish-white shirts made of low-grade cotton, ill-fitting baggy brown denims and jackets, and wooden clogs. There are no socks and no belts for the trousers. The shower attendant has lengths of brown twine hanging around his neck. These are used to hitch up the trousers.

The *clochards* are checked for tuberculosis and herded into the *salon*, a room the size and shape of the central well in a prison. Here they are left. This savage bureaucratic process of depersonalization is the *clochard*'s central experience: to be made less than human, a thing. One cannot attach any blame either to *les bleus* or to the hospital attendants. Yet to witness this process (or, more accurately, processing) is seriously to doubt the right our society has to call itself either civilized or humane. Part of the reason for this is precisely our inability to attach blame to any of the representatives and instigators of this process.

Yet the police themselves recognize that many of the *clochards* are 'characters', a word often used to describe people who are seen as more than normally human, as larger than life. Such recognition makes this kind of processing, which turns people into things, doubly and cruelly ironic.

Until one has witnessed their processing at Nanterre, the *clochards'* efforts to outwit *les bleus* often appear comic, even ludicrous. Afterwards they appear rational and heroic: the heroism of those with few resources.

While the *clochards* were showering, *les bleus* have been playing cards. They have been passing the time, relaxing, waiting out their shift until they can conveniently return to their headquarters on the other side of town.

'Us pair?' Tam shakes his head in mock despair. 'It all started as a joke. We went on a camping holiday on the continent. It was a hoot. And we got to thinking, "Why don't we prolong our stay?" There was nothing for us to go back to. We couldnae stay at home. I mean, the parents are all right, we get along fine. But there's nothing down for the likes of Davy and me with no Highers or anything. It's just waiting for the fortnightly dole cheque, maybe now and then sallying down to the burroo on the off-chance of a job. It was turning our minds to custard.'

It is eleven o'clock at night and they are hauling a flea-blown mattress, found in a doorway off St Germain, back to their pitch under Pont Neuf. 'Aw, we're a dab-hand at the scavenging,' Davy laughs. 'You've got to be in this fucking life. Beg, borrow and steal. That's our motto.'

The evening is hot and sultry. Suddenly, lightning sizzles over their heads and, immediately, rain lashes down. Within a minute the crowded streets are deserted except for the swish of cars and the manic gurgle of the drains. A couple of minutes later Tam and Davy find an awning under which they stack the mattress out of the worst of the rain. They stand looking out at the torrents flooding the roads and pavements. Tam takes a bottle of *vin ordinaire* from his pocket and flips the plastic top in the direction of the gutter.

A quarter of an hour later an ageing hippie stumbles past and collapses face down full length on a bench. Instantly he's asleep in the rain.

'Poor fucker,' Davy commiserates. 'Still, there's always some in every generation who just can't cut the cake.'

'Aye maybe. But you can never tell, Davy. I mean, he looks as though he's had the same old argument battering in his head for ten years. Maybe if that hippie thing hadn't come along just when it did, he'd be a chartered accountant now.'

'True. I can see it now. He's getting along just dandy and he switches on the telly – bit of light relief before the exams – and there's Monty Python making sick jokes about accountants. So he drops a handy tab of acid and short circuits the brainbox.'

'I only hope he's American. I hate the Americans, they're such tight bastards. They're walking donkeys.'

'It's funny, isn't it. We really despise young Americans. But take American books now. Mailer, Kerouac, Hunter Thompson, Henry Miller. Now there you're talking!'

'Aye. We've got them bastards to thank, Davy. Maybe if it wasn't for them we'd be like that poor poloney on the bench. See, we can read something like *On the Road* or *Tropic of Cancer* and for us it's a goldmine. It's not just that it keeps our minds active and buzzing with ideas . . .'

'See we can compare what's happening in the literature with what's happening to us . . .'

'It's like we're part of a tradition. Like the books make our lives make sense.'

'Aw, Jesus, Tam, you're a corker, so you are. And who do you reckon inspired the poor fucker over there? Charles Manson?'

In their reading, Tam and Davy are exceptional. Comics and porn magazines are the usual reading matter of the professional bums. But Tam and Davy are exceptional not just in *what* they read, but in the use that they put their reading to.

By definition, in the classic economic sense of the word, the lives of the *zonards*, bums and *clochards* are non-productive. Against the odds, Tam and Davy are being productive, albeit on the level of the imagination. They are producing meaning and, in so doing, they are shaping the world. They are participating – though in a very restricted way and one that has no influence on others – in the production of the world as reality.

It is this which makes them exceptional and it is this which makes them stand in such sharp contrast to the others in this sub-world of skid row where fantasy can easily take over from harsh reality.

John is a small slight figure waiting to get on the Salvation Army's barge at Pont Austerlitz. Occasionally he tries to jump the queue, but he only succeeds in annoying the other men. 'I've been in France for two weeks. Why am I here? I tried to check in at the Hilton, but it was full up. I'm looking for my girlfriend, actually. She lives in Paris, on the rue Montmartre. You might have heard of her, Sylvia Kristel. I'm going to California to build a ranch so that we can live together . . .'

The ultimate aim of fantasy is to obliterate the world. The effect is to make the individual passive in the face of reality. In John, fantasy had taken over complete control. Because he did not speak a word of French (or, at least, refused to do so) and because the workers at the Salvation Army did not understand a word of English, he was completely marooned from reality.

Some beggars produce in passers-by a state of shock. These are the beggars, a minority, whose posture – whether prostrate or tending towards the foetal position – most expresses utter anguish and total defeat. They reveal themselves as defenceless before the world, while their clothes, their scars, their sores reveal the barbarity of the world they live in. Their attitude is an attitude of surrender.

In the face of this one feels a mixture of physical revulsion, of pity, of guilt and of helplessness. This helplessness may produce outrage. It may produce an immediate refusal to recognize that what is happening is a part of one's own world. No one likes to be presented with evidence of their own inadequacy. In both cases the pedestrian passes by. Or one may distantly recognize one's own helplessness as related to the helplessness of the beggar and produce a coin as a token of that relation.

He zigzags through the strolling, well-heeled crowds, his shabby overcoat trailing open. His shoulders are hunched. His hands, like a bundle of twigs, are clutched in front of his throat. Curly, matted hair and beard straggle around his baby-pink face, which quivers with pain. He zigzags wailing in a high-pitched keen, 'Maman, maman, j'ai perdu ma maman'. An actor couldn't have performed the part of a lost child of under five with more precision or terror. I look into his eyes, then look away quickly before I too become prisoner to the distances and terror they reveal.

--------------------

... In the meantime I worked at the Hôtel X, four days a week in the cafeterie, one day helping the waiter on the fourth floor, and one day replacing the woman who washed up for the dining-room. My day off, luckily, was Sunday, but sometimes another man was ill and I had to work that day as well. The hours were from seven in the morning till two in the afternoon, and from five in the evening till nine – eleven hours; but it was a fourteen-hour day when I washed up for the dining-room. By the ordinary standards of a Paris *plongeur*, these are exceptionally short hours. The only hardship of life was the fearful heat and stuffiness of these labyrinthine cellars. Apart from this the hotel, which was large and well organized, was considered a comfortable one.

Our cafeterie was a murky cellar measuring twenty feet by seven by eight high, and so crowded with coffee-urns, breadcutters and the like that one could hardly move without banging against something. It was lighted by one dim electric bulb, and four or five gas-fires that sent out a fierce red breath. There was a thermometer there, and the temperature never fell below 110 degrees Fahrenheit – it neared 130 at some times of the day. At one end were five service lifts, and at the other was an ice cupboard where we stored milk and butter. When you went into the ice cupboard you dropped a hundred degrees of temperature at a single step; it used to remind me of the hymn about Greenland's icy mountains and India's coral strand. Two men worked in the cafeterie besides Boris and myself. One was Mario, a huge, excitable Italian – he was like a city policeman with operatic gestures – and the other, a hairy, uncouth animal whom we called the Magyar; I think he was a Transylvanian, or something even more remote. Except the Magyar we were all big men, and at the rush hours we collided incessantly.

The work in the cafeterie was spasmodic. We were never idle, but the real work only came in bursts of two hours at a time – we called each burst 'un coup de feu'. The first *coup de feu* came at eight, when the guests upstairs began to wake up and demand breakfast. At eight a sudden banging and yelling would break out all through the basement; bells rang on all sides, blue-aproned men rushed through the passages, our service lifts came down with a simultaneous crash, and the waiters on all five floors began shouting Italian oaths down the shafts. I don't remember all our duties, but they included making tea, coffee and chocolate, fetching meals from the kitchen, wines from the cellar and fruit and so forth from the dining-room, slicing bread, making toast, rolling pats of butter, measuring jam, opening milk-cans, counting lumps of sugar, boiling eggs, cooking porridge, pounding ice, grinding coffee – all this for from a hundred to two hundred customers. The kitchen was thirty yards away, and the dining-room sixty or seventy yards. Everything we sent up in the service lifts had to be covered by a voucher, and the vouchers had to be carefully filed, and there was trouble if even a lump of sugar was lost. Besides this, we had to supply the staff with bread and coffee, and fetch the meals for the waiters upstairs. All in all, it was a complicated job.

I calculated that one had to walk and run about fifteen miles during the day, and yet the strain of the work was more mental than physical. Nothing could be easier, on the face of it, than this stupid scullion work, but it is astonishingly hard when one is in a hurry. One has to leap to and fro between a multitude of jobs – it is like sorting a pack of cards against the clock. You are, for example, making toast, when bang! down comes a service lift with an order for tea, rolls and three different kinds of jam, and simultaneously bang! down comes another demanding scrambled eggs, coffee and grapefruit; you run to the kitchen for the eggs and to the dining-room for the fruit, going like lightning so as to be back before your toast burns, and having to remember about the tea and coffee, besides half a dozen other orders that are still pending; and at the same time some waiter is following you and making trouble about a lost bottle of soda-water, and you are arguing with him. It needs more brains than one might think. Mario said, no doubt truly, that it took a year to make a reliable cafetier.

---

He buys a newspaper most days. Today, with his fellow *clochards* on Place de la Contrescarpe, he reads about yesterday's demonstrations of the medical and pharmacy students in the right wing *Le Figaro*.

'It's a terrible rag, but I prefer to read the other side's lies. It's easier to sort out the truth that way. Besides, it's dispiriting reading lies in your own side's paper.'

A long time ago he joined the Merchant Navy. Like many who have been to sea for a long time, he still, despite everything, retains a trimness to his face and figure, an agility in his walk. He loved the life. Once, in Marseille, he had an anchor tattooed on his forearm.

Despite the regimen of the Navy and the hierarchy on board ship, his constant visits to foreign lands made him an internationalist and a socialist. He visited Poland and the Soviet Union and admired much in those two countries. He visited South Africa and realized that what he valued in each country was the people he met. He was constantly astonished and delighted by the diversity of people, the ways in which they differed from one country to the next. Some day, he hopes, everybody will see the world as he does. Then everyone will have their own governments, distinct nationalities, ways of life. They will still have a place that they can look upon as home. That is very important. But they will also belong to the world, a world without war.

After many happy years in the Navy, he had to retire. The good things in life always come to an end. His mother and father had long since died and he'd lost touch with his other relatives. He came to Paris, became an industrial designer. He was happy, though it wasn't the same as the sea. He never had the urge to marry.

Then there is a period of darkness. He smiles sadly. He shrugs and turns his hands palms up. There are tears in the corners of his eyes. This is something that he cannot bring himself to talk about. '*Je suis tombé*,' he whispers.

Jean, one of his friends, returns from trying on a pair of discarded trousers. 'Much better than the old ones,' he says happily, taking a pull from the communal bottle. An old babushka flaps across the square in her slippers and calls out merrily to one of the *clochard*'s dogs, 'Allô, Sylvie!'

He has recovered himself. 'Look at me, now. It makes me angry. As for Mitterrand! One and a half years he's been in power and look what he's done for us. Nothing! I'm still out on the streets, I still lead the life of a cur. And he calls himself a socialist!'

It's almost seven o'clock in the evening. The sun breaks out briefly over the square. Jean, who has been looking through his postcards – he buys them cheap wholesale for around 30 centimes each then sells them to tourists for two or three francs – gets up. Mousse, a slim, almost dapper companion, returns from an errand he's run for the café on the corner.

'I have to leave you now. It is almost seven o'clock. I have to hide away. *Les bleus* come round looking for us from seven until nine.'

There is a sense in which the individual lives of some *clochards* are like folk-tales, as though even in the midst of the city they preserve something of the rustic. There is another, more solid point of comparison. A common theme of folk-tales is the fate of subjection to spells. The intervention of magic is a metaphor for having one's existence determined by complex, unknown forces. The same is true for Jules, the old *clochard*, both in his original fall and then, later, in his nightly battle of wits against *les bleus*. Of course, not all *clochards* are on the streets because of a sudden dramatic fall. For some it's a gradual process, a slow sinking. Nevertheless, the struggle of the *clochard* is an emblematic struggle, the struggle of the little man against the odds.

'Hey, mind that time on Sauchiehall Street, Davy? Aw, all Glasgae was humming. And us two, we were just another pair of headcases. Banging the hell out of some wee sprite because we didn't like the colour of his scarf. Then weeping all over each other's shoulders. Don't ask me why. It was the only thing to do. All up and doon Sauchiehall Street the same scene was repeating itself, a hundred times over. It doesn't make any sense, does it? It's a wee bit like a pluke. All week the puss is building up inside until it's got a nice wee rosy head. And then you burst it! That's the best bit! God, it fair scunners you but, oh man, the relief!'

'Aye. What I fucking cannae work out is why it's so different here. I mean, here we're on the wine, continuous like. We'll spend the whole evening fucking poncing around the Boulevard St Michel, knocking the stuff back. But it's like we stay just half-drunk all the time. Nice and mellow.'

'Unless those German hard-nuts are up to their tricks again,' Tam nods in the direction of the group next to them under Pont Neuf. 'They're crazy, man.' He passes the bottle of *vin ordinaire* to Davy. 'Getting nostalgic, Davy? He's already thinking of leaving the road. He misses the telly.'

'Aye. *Kojak*. I love it. Pure fucking rubbish.'

'Me, I want to stick it out another five years, then quit while I'm ahead. I don't want to be another stumbling *clochard* – poor blighters.'

Davy finishes the bottle of wine and for a time they lapse into silence. Beside them, the Seine ripples under the bridge. Above, some Americans peer down. Tam flips the top off another bottle of wine. One of the Germans gets up, drops his pants and sticks his bare bum up at the sightseers. It's something he does periodically.

'Hey, Klaus! Come off it, man!' Tam indicates the full bottle of wine. Reluctantly, Klaus hitches up his jeans, buckles his belt, slouches back to his rucksack. Tam waits, then pours a little wine into the Seine. Davy explains: 'An old *clochard* used to kip here. Lovely guy. A few days ago he snoozed off on the river wall. Just over there. He must have turned in his sleep. Anyways, he fell into the Seine and drowned. The top of the wine always goes to him. To remember him by. And so's, wherever he's gone, he's got enough to drink.'

Tam nods and quotes: '"The sun is setting. I feel this river flowing through me – its past, its ancient soil, the changing climate. The hills gently girdle it about: its course is fixed."'

A few *zonards*, though they are loth to admit it, still live with their parents. Others, again only a few, live in cheap hotels, paying their rent monthly. And a few sleep rough.

Les Halles, like all modern public buildings, conforms to stringent fire and safety regulations. Fire exits burrow off from the chic, expensive arcades into unlit concrete corridors and flights of stairs. This is the grotty underside of modernistic Les Halles, the other side of that fashion-conscious universe. Here it makes sense for punks to say that punk is dead: it saves punk from fashion. Fashion is only the other face of death; both signify imminent decay.

Some corners of this nether world smell of piss. Others are lined with cardboard and discarded styrofoam packaging. It is airless, featureless, fetid. It induces paranoia. Because of this, *zonards* use this hideaway as a last resort. They prefer to kip out.

Anyway, most *zonards* don't often need to sleep out. Usually they can find a friend's floor. Or they squat.

Figures vary widely for the number of squatters in Paris. About 3,500 is an educated guess. Numbers fluctuate: in the summer those who've got the energy move to the south of France.

Despite his uncouth appearance, Judes is, in fact, a very gentle person. Like some of the other *zonards* (and most of the general population) he has an exaggerated idea of the violence of the street. One day, fearing that we may be courting danger, he lends us the bodyguard of his group, nicknamed Midi, a burly *zonard* in a blue boilersuit with the ruddy face of a peasant. Once when I was shopping with Midi, I discovered I'd run out of money. Did Midi have any? 'Money?' he replied, smiling vaguely. 'Oh no, I never have any money.'

Judes himself has an insatiable curiosity about how *zonards*, or their equivalent, live in London. He finds the idea of Social Security paying the likes of him intriguing. He can hardly conceive of a licensed squat with full services. It seems like paradise to him. He doesn't quite believe it. 'It's funny,' he says. 'I lived all my life in Le Touquet. It's nearer London than Paris, yet I've never been to England. I'd like to go to London. Maybe I'll go there this summer ...' That doesn't seem likely. He decides, instead, to go to the south of France for the summer. Two days later, he is back again.

Judes's squat is a mess. It is a condemned building, made derelict when the council stripped out the plumbing, the electricity, the doors, the windows. It has been made unfit for human habitation with a passionate bureaucratic thoroughness. One floor, the top floor, is used as their living quarters. There is no security, but here at least they are able to hear the police coming up the stairs. The police have already visited them twice: Paris loathes squatters. One room is used for living in, one for sleeping. Five people live here. There is a third room used by another couple, squatters also, who cook food over logs on the concrete floor and who, Judes and his clique suspect, have recently started thieving from them. The smell in the room is awful: fierce, ripe and cheesy. The floor below is used as a toilet: one room is littered with strangely naked-looking dried-up human turds. Oddly, this room doesn't smell bad at all.

'It's hell of a dirty, it really stinks,' Judes apologizes. Yet he is proud and happy to invite strangers to his home. He is a believer in hospitality.

The afternoon passes slowly. Tante and Yvonne darn clothes. Joie tells everyone's fortunes; they are all intensely superstitious. To enter their world is to enter a world where appeals cannot be made to moral codes. There is no framework in which such an appeal could be understood.

Appeals can, however, be made to superstition. One can excuse oneself from a certain expected action by appeal to superstition. One's destiny is in the hands of Fate.

Their world is a world bereft of the possibility of human choice. They wear the same clothes, like the same music, use the same drugs as the original hippies, but unlike them they are not themselves any part of social change. They are only vaguely ecologist; though this may be more a reflection of their superstition, their anti-rationalistic outlook.

Judes takes his foot out of his boot and examines it critically. He believes that the bone in his big toe is cracked. It is very painful but he refuses to go to the hospital. The procedure to obtain free treatment is too complicated, he says. Instead he bends his boot backwards and forwards to make the leather more supple. His boots are new: thieved from a fancy boutique near the Pompidou Centre.

About six Tante and Yvonne go out shopping. When they return they fetch out butter and chocolate they have hidden among their clothes. 'How else do you expect us to eat?' inquires Tante. The bread has been bought. It is almost impossible to steal the long French bread.

Carefully, the bread is broken into equal quantities, the butter and chocolate unwrapped. They are attentive first to the needs of their guests. Only after these have been satisfied do they construct their own chocolate sandwiches, the crunchy chocolate bar layered two, even three, slabs thick. Then they eat. I realize that they are, quite literally, famished.

Marc and Marcel return laden down with wine, beer, food. And with hash. 'This daft student came up to us, asking if we knew where to score,' Marc explains, switching off his Walkman. 'We took him round the back of Beaubourg. There's a fire escape, a dead end, by the new flats. We told him we'd beat him up if he didn't hand over his money. Poor sod, he was pissing himself. The creep didn't even know the going rate. He had two hundred francs. We took his money and scarpered . . .'

'Went round and scored with a hundred francs and spent the rest on this stuff,' Marcel breaks in. 'We're celebrating.' Dramatic pause. 'I've got let off National Service.' He laughs, delighted. 'I wrote to the commanding officer of the unit I was going to serve in, saying that I'd fucked his wife and she was a lousy cunt. He's written back saying that I won't be required for military service, that I'm unsuitable material, and that he's locked up his wife.' For a moment he becomes uncharacteristically wistful. 'Now all I need is a girlfriend, a girlfriend like you, Joie.'

All evening, when he's not crashed out with dope, he mimics the student quaking with terror and the commanding officer quaking with anger.

Everyone gorges, everyone gets drunk and stoned, everyone parties. Their world isn't constructed out of the same categories as ours: work, home and family life, hobbies and leisure, political and religious beliefs. It is a world caught in the present. Only in the love between Judes and Joie is the presence of the future acknowledged. Their love acts as a mascot for the group. It opens up the possibility of a future, it becomes an avenue of hope.

Yet to imagine a future is to reinsert the categories we live by: work, family life, leisure, etc. The *zonards* cannot find the key to unlock themselves from the present. It is as though they are in a prison without walls.

In the middle of the evening there is a furious slanging match. 'We are always having this argument,' Tante explains. 'We all like each other and get on well with each other. And we all want to leave Paris, Paris drags you down. I'm older than the rest, I'm twenty-seven, so perhaps I notice it more, but I keep thinking that I can't go on living in this way. I don't know why, but I think we're getting more violent. We are all good with our hands, quite skilled. So we talk about finding somewhere in the country and settling down there. All together: a commune. But the problem is that Joie is still a minor. If she came with us now we could be accused of kidnapping. So we argue about whether we go now without Joie and she joins us in two years' time, or whether we all wait here for two years. It's a great problem.'

A month later the group was disintegrating. Marc and Judes had fallen out and Marc was off to Brittany where he hoped to pick up summer work as a deck-hand on a chartered yacht. Yvonne couldn't decide whether to stay or go with him. Joie had been sent to a stricter boarding school which she could escape from only at weekends. And, one day, Marcel met a Dutch *zonard*, a huge fellow. This was just before the date of his call-up. The next day he announced that he was off with his friend to Amsterdam. The day after, he disappeared.

Everyone joked about it: Marcel would never have got further than the Périphérique; it would be a bloody miracle if he got as far as the Belgian border. But everyone was worried: it was too easy to get hold of drugs in Amsterdam, they were too available and too cheap. No one was prepared to say he couldn't handle that scene; but they all thought he was too young, too crazy.

Down Les Halles times were getting tough. The police were becoming much heavier. Heroin was beginning to come in cheap. People were spending more time outside, by the fountain. Two black guys organized boxing bouts there. These were supposed to be sporting contests, and afterwards the hat was passed round for the volunteer boxers. But Georges kept insisting on fighting, and after a few minutes he always started to fight seriously. The cool rastas who used to hang out on the second floor of Les Halles did a flit, and everybody started wondering if that was a sign. But no one knew for sure.

# London

Last year, London's evening newspaper, the *Standard*, put the figure of homeless people in London at 50,000. This is the size of a small town, Tunbridge Wells or Shrewsbury for instance. Imagine such a town, the town with a population of 50,000, or thereabouts, that you know best. Imagine it bustling and alive, the rhythms of daily life, its shops and markets and factories and offices, its High Street and its small friendly rush hours. Imagine it in as much detail and with as much affection as possible.

Now imagine it completely deserted, like the Marie Celeste. No men, no women, no young people, no old people. Absent, disappeared into the diaspora of skid row. Skid row – a largely unseen world of rotting, deserted slums (called 'skips'), of Victorian lodging houses and institutional hostels, of crash-pads, night shelters, squats, friends' floors and seedy bed-and-breakfast hotels.

'I hit this place first when I was seventeen. I'm sixty-eight now and that was fifty years ago.' Taff comes from Pontypridd, wears a check sports jacket and grey corduroy trousers. A triangle of white handkerchief is set carefully in his breast pocket. For three years he has been living in Arlington House, one of the chain of Rowton Houses. It is a vast Victorian hostel, dingy and decaying, with cell-like wooden partitioned rooms for over a thousand men. Over on the other side of the dimly lit games room two men bend over a once handsome billiard table. Taff continues, 'I started off as a miner. Now that's the worst thing, going down the pit. Now then, that first time as the lift goes down, it takes the belly out of you. Down into the darkness. I went down at fourteen. It was because of my parents' attitude which was basically, "We've kept you for fourteen years, now get out and work." So there I was, standing at the top as the shift went down, saying, "Do you want a boy?" to each man as he passed. I tell you, I got out of there as quick as I could. I came to London at seventeen. Eventually, I joined the Army. I'd ended up chopping wood for a bowl of soup. And when I joined the Army I didn't even have a jacket. I'd pawned the jacket. After the Army, I lived in Aldershot. Then my marriage broke up...' (Taff's mate, Scouser, interrupts here, 'This fucking world, it's organized wrong. Completely back to front. He and his wife don't get on, so he lands up here. With me, I'm here because my wife is lying buried in a hole in the ground. The dearest heart that ever lived, she was. Now then, why didn't Taff's wife die instead of mine? Then we'd both be happy, both still at home.') 'Well, as I said, my marriage broke up. So I packed my job in, I was a crane driver at the time, and at sixty-two I came to London to start a new life!'

He lies curled in a corner of Euston Station. He is still in his teens, a skinhead; been in London for five weeks. His feet have blistered inside his shoes. His mate, a much older man, counsels: 'The feet, now, is half your battle. As long as your feet are set up, you're all right for this business.' James, the skinhead, limps across the concourse. 'My parents threw me out. I'd lost my job, I'd been working in a bakery. Well, that's what they called it, chemical factory more like. I was always getting nicked, like I knew all the fiddles on the fruit machines. Me mum and dad were tired of the police always coming round. I thought, anywhere must be better than this place. And I suppose I also reckoned all that corny stuff about streets paved with gold.' He drinks the strong Bovril soup provided by the Salvation Army soup run. ('We soon find out what goes down well,' George, the soup-maker and driver, informs us. 'I trained as a chef. I tried them out on leek soup one run, but they weren't having any of that.') When offered, James accepts another cup of soup, then retreats to a corner out of the wind which always seems to swirl around the new Euston Station office blocks. 'Sometimes I wonder about going back home.' His mate interrupts, 'Ah now, there you're talking! I wish you could argue some sense into the lad. He's too young for this kind of life.' 'I don't know if I want to. I don't know if my parents would take me back. But maybe I'll go, have a rest, do a few fruit machines. Then come back here with my mate.'

'What's the difference between the Scottish and the Welsh, and the Irish?' Shaun pauses for a fraction of a second. The light from the single candle in his skip, a condemned and boarded-up tenement, dances in his eye. Peter, bronchitic, coughs feebly from the mattress on the floor and sucks at the shared can of Special Brew. Dark patches of mould grow on the peeling wallpaper, the tide-mark of rising damp is four, even five, feet high in places. The house cat rubs herself against Shaun's legs. Shaun crackles on with his joke, 'The Irishman can't walk home . . .' At times, Shaun jokes too much. It is as though he uses his joking as a defence, as walls behind which he can hide. 'Well, how do you like home, eh? Home, sweet home. Running water – down the walls . . . You want to know how I got here? My wife died and I had a fight with my brother at the funeral. After that, my sons kicked me out, kicked me out of my own house. They're only living two hundred yards up the road, but they don't want anything to do with me. I could be living on a different universe.' He lights up a cigarette, hands it to Peter. Lights up another for himself and launches into another joke.

*

'My parents live in a beautiful little cottage, about four hundred years old, grey stone and all that. It's lovely. Well, a lovely place for a holiday. It's in this tiny village. There's a castle about a hundred yards down the road, it's quite famous. They get lots of coachloads from Birmingham and places like that. After they've snapped the castle, the tourists stroll down and stand at my mum's front door and say, "Oh, a real olde English cottage with real olde English peasants." ' Alison mimics the tourists' attempts at a peasant accent. She is eighteen, wears a teeshirt, jeans and trainers, lives on Social Security in a shabby bed-and-breakfast hotel in Earl's Court. Her room, which she shares with Audrey, a black seventeen-year-old originally from Shepherd's Bush, has been partitioned off from a back corridor in the hotel. The stud-wall between room and corridor reaches to no more than two feet above the top of the door. Together, they pay £70 rent per week. 'My dad is a manager in a big firm. He's quite important, earns about £25,000 a year. He's all right ... When I was a kid I ran away from home a number of times. They tried everything on me. I went to approved school once. It was terrible. You were locked in your dormitory even though it was supposed to be open. I remember when we used to have games. There was this walkway between two blocks of the school and the staff would line up there with cricket bats and tennis rackets and make cracks at you, just tempting you to make a run for it ... I suppose I just went from one thing to another, from bad to worse. But I just couldn't stand home, the way my parents lived. It was suffocating, stifling, unreal. When I ran away, I wasn't doing nothing wrong, I was just saying that I didn't want to live like that ... I'm eighteen now, old enough to make up my own mind.'

Some men play cards on the institutional formica-topped tables, others read or talk in scraps of conversation. One stringy old man sits by himself, cracking his fingers. Very gently he sings to himself an old Scottish playground chant: 'Here we sit like birds in the wilderness, birds in the wilderness, birds in the wilderness ...' The common room, like the dormitories upstairs, is almost clinically clean, its bareness interrupted only by notices and regulations. The smell is reminiscent – except that it is more piercing and overburdened with stale sweat and other bodily effluvia – of that in a geriatric hospital, only minus the smells of medication and the occasional bunch of flowers: there are no visitors at the Salvation Army hostel. Mr John speaks, a curious throaty sound: 'I won't hear a word against this place. It suits me fine. It's clean and you know exactly where you are. There's no malarkey ... How did I come here? Oh, that's easy. Spat out of the Army after thirty years' service. That was the worst time in my life. The Army just doesn't equip you for life. They chuck you out, they don't see you're vulnerable. I was lost, I was like a bairn. I had nowhere to stay, no job and I landed up here. Oh, I know ...' For the first time a wry, half-mocking smile floods into his hooded grey eyes. 'From the British Army to the Salvation Army. I'm no so keen with the big words but I know what's happening. I'm no dumdum. Most of the chaps here aren't. Don't imagine we don't have feelings, you all think we don't have feelings . . . Anyway, like I said, it suits me fine this place. You've got to have discipline.'

When he left school he got a job as a technician in an animal laboratory. After a few months he suddenly realized what he was doing: that the process he was part of was designed to test the safety of cosmetics for humans but had the effect of killing and maiming many hundreds of animals. 'I was brewing the tea and it clicked. There I was, doing the same experiment over and over again, production-line stuff. Then counting the number of stiffs to see if the chemical was poisonous. So it wasn't that the job was just useless. It was worse. And even though I'm not a great rat fan . . .' Unable to find suitable words, Chummie shrugs, then bends down and warms his hands by the one-bar electric fire. The narrow hotel room is stifling. The curtains are permanently drawn across the window. The atmosphere is claustrophobic. 'I poured the tea out for everyone. They all had their own mugs. Then I went along the corridor and handed in my notice. The boss argued with me. "You'll never get another job," he said. I said, "I couldn't care less." ' Later, after he'd left, he returned and 'did the place. I let all the animals out of their cages. It was good . . . Except that the police nicked me for it.' He came to London. 'I was already starting out on junk before I left the lab. Maybe it was sticking all those needles into animals that gave me the idea.' He became a junkie. Then he was sent to prison. Released, he returned to London and tried to find a job. After looking without success for a few months he came to believe that he would never find one. He decided that work, anyway, wasn't desirable, wasn't worth the hassle.

The concrete ramps and pathways crisscross, connecting the different blocks of flats that make up the Haygate Estate. Like many local post-war council developments, it is already decaying. The tenants – those who can afford to – are moving out. This is not one of those estates where people wants to buy their own council house, but one where the lifts are always broken and only the graffiti blossoms. Robert points to a curtainless fifth-floor window: 'That's the next matchbox we've got marked out. As soon as the council chuck us out of this squat, we'll flit over there . . . No, I never thought I'd end up in this mess. I was three years in the Army, including two tours of Northern Ireland. I got out and the next day I'd started on an apprenticeship in electronics with Decca in Battersea. I was on holiday when the factory closed down. Came back to my cards. And pretty soon, since I don't accept dole from anyone, I had nowhere to stay.'

Winston looks at me with sly good humour. 'Yes, I'm different, I'm here by choice,' he drawls. 'I come from a good family and I can always get out.

I have the ability. I haven't a drink or drugs problem. I'm not withdrawn. The life isn't bad. I find I meet a lot of different types of people here, some of them are quite characters.' Winston lives under the Queen Elizabeth Hall by the Thames with a small loose-knit group of friends. Duncan, for instance, is a motorbike messenger who couldn't afford to rent a bedsitter. For the time being he is working and saving his money in a building society. Next year he hopes to have enough to put down as a deposit on a flat. Winston has no such plans. He is content to drift. 'There's a certain amount of freedom here,' he discourses. 'It's not run of the mill. I've been a kitchen porter, a gardener, I've been to college. Now, I've opted out. I scavenge. It's surprising how few people will go down bins.' The damp from the Thames creeps through the shadowy concrete bunker; the wind eddies, scribbles a graffiti of cigarette ends, ticket stubs, ice-cream wrappings and dirt across the floor, and brings a fleeting exhalation of urine and disinfectant. For a moment, his hobo good humour deserts him: 'This is the type of environment that if you don't keep your spirits up, you get depressed. You only need to look at some of the older guys. Some of them are only forty yet they look about seventy.'

The open fire at Spitalfields Market flares and a sooty flame bellows up. Though not so much these days as formerly, Spitalfields Market is a source of casual work for homeless men and the fire on the north side of the yard is a gathering place for dossers. A large catering tin of baked beans with two holes punched in the lid bubbles and boils by the side of the fire. Paddy sits on the low wall beside the fire, drinking cider. 'I come over here twenty fuckin' year ago. An' I've been skipperin' out for twenty fuckin' year and, by the grace of de Almighty, I'll be skipperin' out for another twenty fuckin' year. It's a grand life. I have been wid all classes of men, I have worked for Wimpey, McAlpine, the lot, and I tell you your dosser is the decentest of all men . . . Why did I leave de Emerald Isle? Dey make you work seven fuckin' days a week over dere. Here you can drink seven fuckin' days a week.' With that, he returns to his bottle.

Like thousands of young Irish men and women, Paddy was forced to leave Ireland because of its underdevelopment and the acute shortage of jobs. In England and London he found employment, but in the process he lost something else. It is usual to say of people like Paddy that he escaped from the stifling pressures of rigid Catholicism and conformity. He, himself, in his tales of nuns 'in the home country' may appear to reinforce that impression. For him, though, it makes some sort of emotional sense to try to convert a deep personal loss into a gain, to make escape out of eviction. For us, to think that he escaped is to deceive ourselves and to misconstrue history.

In 1903 it was estimated that 30,000 people were homeless in London. The next thirty years brought increasing prosperity to the United Kingdom.

In 1933 it was estimated that nearly 30,000 people were homeless in London. Once again, the next fifty years brought vastly increasing prosperity to the United Kingdom. In 1983 it was estimated that 50,000 were homeless in London. Some of this increase may be journalistic exaggeration; some may be because nowadays we categorize certain people as homeless who were formerly regarded as housed. Nevertheless, it is a bleak statistic.

It is made bleaker by recent analysis which shows that there is a direct correlation between homelessness and unemployment. The former increases directly with the latter. And when unemployment decreases, so too does homelessness. Pundits (employed) pontificate about society having to learn to live with long-term structural unemployment, with the new age of enforced leisure. They ignore the fact that what unemployment brings is homelessness. This is the reverse of leisure. It is the black economy of despair.

And homelessness doesn't discriminate. Statistics for homeless families show that about one third have never known secure accommodation, one fifth last lived in council rented property, and a similar proportion in private rented property. One in ten had had accommodation with their job. And about 15 per cent had been owner-occupiers. (This book does not deal with homeless families, but with sections of the single homeless, of whom statistics are not kept. Nevertheless, the proportions seem broadly correct.)

In some ways the homeless can be compared to refugees. Refugees are those people who have been forced to flee their homes because of civil war, invasion, natural disaster – certainly through no fault of their own. Similarly, most people who become homeless do not elect to come to London of their own free will. They, like the majority who come to London and find homes, are migrants searching for work, hoping for a better life.

It is difficult to underestimate the extent of migration under the industrial capitalism of the last two centuries. In England in the early nineteenth century, for instance, agents of the Poor Law Commission scoured the South West for recruits for the burgeoning factories of Manchester. After the Irish Potato Famine of 1845–7 (when English land policies had destroyed the structure of Irish agriculture by transforming it from subsistence farming to grain-based cash crops for export), hundreds of thousands of Irish peasants were dispersed to Liverpool and Glasgow to work, as immigrants, in casual labouring jobs. In the Highlands of Scotland a vigorous, broad-based peasant and fishing society was destroyed and replaced first with sheep farming and then later with deer. The Highlands was turned by the rich into a playground for the rich. Scottish soldiers returning home from the Crimea found their villages razed, their families emigrated or disappeared. They, in turn, migrated to Glasgow and to the other industrial centres.

The history of this century is the same, except that migration has increased and labour has been drawn from all parts of the world, from the West Indies, the Indian sub-continent and other parts of the Commonwealth. The work-permit system, which grew up during the sixties and was originally intended to fill the requirement for skilled employment, has brought unskilled labour (after pressure from employers) from the Phillipines, Turkey and Latin America.

At the same time, the regions and countries from which the workers have been drawn have become underdeveloped. This underdevelopment is no longer confined to the Third World. Towns and cities and areas of cities in Britain, mainly in the north of England and in Scotland and Wales, have now fallen into a form of underdevelopment whose structures are more akin to the Third World than the First. With the decay, social and economic, of these areas, the reasons for staying there diminish. A vicious cycle begins. More and more people leave, drawn by the magnet of London. Only London, the metropolitan centre, can fill the vacuum left by the underdevelopment of their hometown. As more people leave, the underdevelopment accelerates, forcing further people out. Yet this London is as much a mirage as a geographical location. There is another London, the London of the inner-city wasteland and the suburban desert. This London is prey to underdevelopment. It, too, suffers from 'emigration' and displacement.

Most of the people who come to London find jobs and homes. They are the fortunate ones, the ones with enough money in their pockets, with friends and contacts who can help them through the initial difficult period, with jobs waiting for them.

For the others, those who rapidly become homeless, their escape from their underdeveloped hometowns turns sour. By becoming homeless, the new arrivals to London fall from being victims at one level of underdevelopment to being victims at a lower level. Their acts of courage and individual striving have been defeated. Without money, they feel dwarfed by the immensity of London; for this is no longer the tourist London of Eros, Harrods and Oxford Street, but the London of innumerable Social Security offices, employment exchanges and job centres separated by an interminable maze of pavements and sudden petty regulations. It is a London whose scale is measured by foot, not by taxi, tube, car or bus. They feel alone, almost as though they are in a foreign land. And they become dislocated in time as well as in place. The past becomes cut off from the present.

Though at the moment of leaving their hometown they had felt that their departure was at least partly their own decision, they now begin to realize how heavily the odds have been stacked: the lack of a job, the miserable social and leisure facilities, the crowded matchbox house where they always felt they were on top of their parents/friends/spouse – all these have conspired to make their decision, somehow, inevitable.

It begins to make sense when they compare themselves with the Vietnamese Boat People. They, too, have been forced to flee their homes, as they would see it, through no fault of their own.

Once in London, they learn to cope as best they can, learn to scrape a living somehow in the complicated world of homelessness, learn to make a little money, legal or illegal. They try not to get dragged down.

————

The eight shillings lasted three days and four nights. After my bad experience in the Waterloo Road I moved eastward, and spent the next night in a lodging-house in Pennyfields. This was a typical lodging-house, like scores of others in London. It had accommodation for between fifty and a hundred men, and was managed by a 'deputy' – a deputy for the owner, that is, for these lodging-houses are profitable concerns and are owned by rich men. We slept fifteen or twenty in a dormitory; the beds were again cold and hard, but the sheets were not more than a week from the wash, which was an improvement. The charge was ninepence or a shilling (in the shilling dormitory the beds were six feet apart instead of four) and the terms were cash down by seven in the evening or out you went.

Downstairs there was a kitchen common to all lodgers, with free firing and a supply of cooking-pots, tea-basins and toasting-forks. There were two great clinker fires, which were kept burning day and night the year through. The work of tending the fires, sweeping the kitchen and making the beds was done by the lodgers in rotation. One senior lodger, a fine Norman-looking stevedore named Steve, was known as 'head of the house', and was arbiter of disputes and unpaid chucker-out.

I liked the kitchen. It was a low-ceiled cellar deep underground, very hot and drowsy with coke fumes, and lighted only by the fires, which cast black velvet shadows in the corners. Ragged washing hung on strings from the ceiling. Red-lit men, stevedores mostly, moved about the fires with cooking-pots; some of them were quite naked, for they had been laundering and were waiting for their clothes to dry. At night there were games of nap and draughts, and songs – 'I'm a chap what's done wrong by my parents', was a favourite, and so was another popular song about a shipwreck. Sometimes late at night men would come in with a pail of winkles they had bought cheap, and share them out. There was a general sharing of food, and it was taken for granted to feed men who were out of work. A little pale, wizened creature, obviously dying, referred to as 'pore Brown, bin under the doctor and cut open three times,' was regularly fed by the others.

Two or three of the lodgers were old-age pensioners. Till meeting them I had never realized that there are people in England who live on nothing but the old-age pension of ten shillings a week. None of these old men had any other resource whatever. One of them was talkative and I asked him how he managed to exist. He said:

'Well, there's ninepence a night for yer kip – that's five an threepence a week. Then there's threepence on Saturday for a shave – that's five an' six. Then say you 'as a 'aircut once a month for sixpence – that's another three'apence a week. So you 'as about four an' fourpence for food an' bacca.'

He could imagine no other expenses. His food was bread and margarine and tea – towards the end of the week dry bread and tea without milk – and perhaps he got his clothes from charity. He seemed contented, valuing his bed and fire more than food. But, with an income of ten shillings a week, to spend money on a shave – it is awe-inspiring.

————

Alison and Audrey's room is the unofficial social centre for many of the unemployed youth who live in the bed-and-breakfast hotels which have multiplied in Earl's Court over the past twenty years. People come to chat, to show off their latest tattoos, to see if anyone knows where to score barbs or other drugs, or simply to crash out. This afternoon a friend of Audrey's is sleeping on one bed and another is lying in a half-comatose state over the other. Two more friends, punks, are killing time until the evening when there's a concert at the Brixton Ace. Alison is half-admiring a new top that Audrey has turned up with. The talk is desultory. The television drones on during the gaps, though hardly anyone pays it much attention. (Once in Chummie's room the television played almost completely through *Parliamo Italiano* before Tim, Chummie's room-mate, noticed. 'What's that fucking thing doing on?' he grumbled, but no one bothered even to switch channels.)

The television – always black and white – is on constantly in all the rooms of all the shabby hotels which depend for their profits on the supplementary benefits that these unemployed youth claim from the Department of Health and Social Security (DHSS). It is the one luxury the hotels provide. It helps to establish a sense of living in the continuous present, a sense of time where not only the past but also the future have been divorced from the present.

It is switched on first thing in the morning by those who are awake, though few are awake: the morning is the dead time of the day. Besides, 'What's the point of going down to breakfast?' Alison murmurs. 'We go down about once a week. Sometimes they have run out of bread, so there's no toast. Sometimes the milkman hasn't arrived, so there's no tea.'

Most hotels which cater for the DHSS trade supply bed and breakfast for the simple reason that the DHSS allowances for bed-and-breakfast accommodation are considerably higher than for lodging alone. And there are few checks to ensure that the hotels maintain a reasonable standard. Most of these hotels charge a pound or two over the local DHSS maximum (the rates vary from town to town) thereby ensuring that pressure is maintained on the DHSS to raise their maximum. It is a form of extortion.

Alison and Audrey's hotel is, for the most part, typical of these hotels. The foyer is plush: red fitted carpets, good-quality flock wallpaper, a handsome imitation antique chandelier and a browser rack of brochures for Covent Garden opera and theatreland. A young Australian woman sits behind the reception desk reading a bestselling paperback.

The foyer and the pleasant Australian are, however, mainly for show. The original Victorian rooms have been divided into two, often three narrow billets and even the smallest and dingiest of these berths is designated 'a double'. Though there is nothing definitively squalid about these rooms, the facilities are few, hot water irregular or non-existent, the windows grimy, the threadbare off-cuts of riotously patterned carpet unhoovered and the beds remain unmade. In Alison and Audrey's room the one article of decoration is a copy of an eighteenth-century cartoon in a heavy, scratched frame depicting a foundling being carried off by two prosperous wives. Perhaps it is the owner's joke: there is a pervasive atmosphere of transitoriness about the room. It is the kind of hotel room one can imagine putting up with for a night, if dusk has caught one in a strange town still miles from one's destination.

The owner of this hotel is rumoured to own other hotels around Earl's Court, but he operates through a management company and is unlocatable. No one has ever seen him and his total staff is rumoured to consist of the Australian receptionist and a Turkish manager. Everything is organized to maximize the owner's profits. He exploits not only his guests (and, through the DHSS, all who pay taxes) but also his workers. He relies on their desire to stay in Britain and their illegal status to pay them as little as possible. In return he turns a blind eye to their laziness or other foibles.

The hotel has thirty-five rooms and is usually full, mostly with youth on supplementary benefits. They pay upwards of £30 rent per week each. They prefer this hotel to others in the area because the manager doesn't bother them when they have visitors in their rooms and because, at least in Alison and Audrey's case, he never tries to solicit them. Meanwhile the owner has an income in excess of £100,000 per year and outgoings of probably less than half that. It is a profitable trade. There is money, easy money to be made out of homelessness.

This afternoon they're all killing time. It's Thursday, but for some reason there's been a delay in all their giro cheques. No one has any money. Everyone is hungry, on edge. The televison rumbles on, an endless procession of *News*, *Nationwide*, *Crossroads*, *Tomorrow's World*. No one pays much heed until *Top of the Pops*: only this engages their attention. They are all *aficionados* of pop. They trade facts about the stars' lives. They are critical about the studio audience's fashions. They swap opinions: some · like Bonnie Tyler, others The Style Council. Some want punk, others Bucks Fizz. Their tastes are amazingly diverse.

Of the group in the room, most had been in conflict with their parents. It is often assumed that the young come from the provinces. Yet they also come from the suburbs of London and London itself. The provinces isn't so much a geographical location as an expression of the attitudes of their elders. What adult mainstream society doesn't realize emotionally is that the tramlines which lead from education to a job with prospects to courtship, marriage, a better job with better prospects are an archaeological curiosity. Trams no longer run on them. Worse, mainstream society doesn't realize that the gap between its beliefs and reality constitutes an act of violence to, and rejection of, its children.

When the programme finishes everyone feels deflated. Alison tells them all to scram. Her mother and younger sister are coming up to London the next day and she wants to take them out for a treat. Her sister has always wanted to go to Madame Tussauds.

'I'm working tonight,' she laughs, ironically. 'I say "I'm working" because it sounds better than "going on the game"! Last night was a washout. I played cat and mouse with the police all night, up and down Park Lane. I prefer it up there to here. I only do blow-jobs. Ten minutes and a shake. I can get forty or fifty quid in an hour. There was this bloke wanted to come down on me. I hate the thought of that, it sends shivers up and down my spine. I said, "No way." I shouldn't be doing this, you know. The politicians should come down here and see what's happening. It's not so bad for me, but there's girls of thirteen, fourteen on the game. I reckon about eighty per cent of the girls down here are on the game. It's terrible.'

Suddenly she bursts into tears. Her whole body quakes. Her anguish overwhelms her and returns her to her childhood. For long moments she is inconsolable. At times like these the adult belief in second chances seems fatuous.

After a time she recovers. She thinks that perhaps it all started to go wrong when she was younger, when she was raped by an older man, an acquaintance of the family. It was, she says, a particularly nasty incident. 'That's one of the reasons I really hate the police,' she says, 'because when I reported it they said things like "I bet you really liked it, you slut." They said it was my own fault because I was hitch-hiking at the time ... There I go again. It must really get boring. Everybody's conversation around here is always about just three things: the drugs they've scored, the punters they've pulled or the run-ins they've had with the police.'

The youth like Alison and Audrey and their friends tend to stay in their hotel rooms. They retreat into themselves, into drugs and into the black-and-white fantasy of the television. For the older, usually male, hostel-dweller and dosser the reality is different. They are forced out of their hostel room or dormitory early in the morning and forbidden to return until late afternoon. There is no rational reason why the hostel authorities do this: hotel guests, after all, are not required to vacate their rooms for eight hours a day so that they may be cleaned and the bed made. The sole purpose – whether the hostel is commercial or run by the local council or by the Salvation Army makes no difference – is to assert the superiority of the hostel staff and owners and to remind the hostel-dweller of his insecurity.

The hostel-dweller is often unemployed or retired, yet in some awful parody and pretence at work he is forced to take to the streets between nine and five. He goes on the circuit. The world of the homeless is full of circuits. There is the daily circuit of streets, sleazy cafés, day centres, library reading-rooms. For those less fortunate there is the circuit of handouts. There are institutional circuits: from one voluntary agency to the next; from a Salvation Army hostel to the government resettlement centre or 'spike'; from a local council emergency night shelter (where he may stay only three nights after which period he is no longer classified as an emergency) to a Simon Community crash-pad. He is passed from police to prison to probation officer to social worker. He has to sign on at offices solely for the homeless. He becomes lost in a maze of forms administered by officious bureaucrats. He goes from the bottle to one of the few de-tox units to the bottle again. Some have come to London to escape the consequences of a crime they have committed – or, as is more likely, a crime they believe they have committed, for the crimes are often as much imagined as real. Yet their way of life, their constant contacts with the police, only reinforce their belief that they must at one time have committed a crime, since they are now branded as criminals.

It is a world where time has stopped, where the past is denied and the future ruled out of bounds. And it is a world where all the officials, in word, deed or attitude, confirm the homeless individual in his belief that if there is anything wrong it is because he is at fault.

It is a world a little like a *Monopoly* board: it is remorseless. There is nowhere to get off, though you can go round it fast or slow; occasionally you get sent to jail; occasionally you land on Free Parking; most often you're paying out rent (all the property has been bought up long before). It's a game you can never win, even the Chance cards are loaded against you.

---

Paddy was my mate for about the next fortnight, and, as he was the first tramp I had known at all well, I want to give an account of him. I believe that he was a typical tramp and there are tens of thousands in England like him.

He was a tallish man, aged about thirty-five, with fair hair going grizzled and watery blue eyes. His features were good, but his cheeks had lanked and had that greyish, dirty in the grain look that comes of a bread and margarine diet. He was dressed, rather better than most tramps, in a tweed shooting-jacket and a pair of old evening trousers with the braid still on them. Evidently the braid figured in his mind as a lingering scrap of respectability, and he took care to sew it on again when it came loose. He was careful of his appearance altogether, and carried a razor and bootbrush that he would not sell, though he had sold his 'papers' and even his pocket-knife long since. Nevertheless, one would have known him for a tramp a hundred yards away. There was something in his drifting style of walk, and the way he had of hunching his shoulders forward, essentially abject. Seeing him walk, you felt instinctively that he would sooner take a blow than give one.

He had been brought up in Ireland, served two years in the war, and then worked in a metal polish factory, where he had lost his job two years earlier. He was horribly ashamed of being a tramp, but he had picked up all a tramp's ways. He browsed the pavements unceasingly, never missing a cigarette end, or even an empty cigarette packet, as he used the tissue paper for rolling cigarettes. On our way into Edbury he saw a newspaper parcel on the pavement, pounced on it, and found that it contained two mutton sandwiches, rather frayed at the edges; these he insisted on my sharing. He never passed an automatic machine without giving a tug at the handle for he said sometimes they are out of order and will eject pennies if you tug at them. He had no stomach for crime, however. When we were in the outskirts of Romton, Paddy noticed a bottle of milk on a doorstep, evidently left there by mistake. He stopped, eyeing the bottle hungrily.

'Christ!' he said, 'dere's good food goin' to waste. Somebody could knock dat bottle off, eh? Knock it off easy.'

I saw that he was thinking of 'knocking it off' himself. He looked up and down the street; it was a quiet residential street and there was nobody in sight. Paddy's sickly, chap-fallen face yearned over the milk. Then he turned away, saying gloomily:

'Best leave it. It don't do a man no good to steal. T'ank God, I ain't never stolen nothin' yet.'

It was funk, bred of hunger, that kept him virtuous. With only two or three sound meals in his belly, he would have found courage to steal the milk.

He had two subjects of conversation, the shame and come-down of being a tramp, and the best way of getting a free meal. As we drifted through the streets he would keep up a monologue in this style, in a whimpering, self-pitying Irish voice...

Self-pity was the clue to his character. The thought of his bad luck never seemed to leave him for an instant. He would break long silences to exclaim, apropos of nothing, 'It's hell when yer clo'es begin to go up de spout, eh?' or 'Dat tay in de spike ain't tay, it's piss,' as though there was nothing else in the world to think about. And he had a low, worm-like envy of anyone who was better off - not of the rich, for they were beyond his social horizon, but of men in work. He pined for work as an artist pines to be famous. If he saw an old man working he would say bitterly 'Look at dat old — keepin' able-bodied men out o' work'; or if it was a boy, 'It's dem young devils what's takin' de bread out of our mouths.' And all foreigners to him were 'dem bloody dagoes' - for, according to his theory, foreigners were responsible for unemployment.

---

'It must have been the third or fourth night after I'd been slung out,' Shaun reminisces. 'By Jesus, it must have been the coldest night I've ever been through. It's a wonder I got through that mudder-fugger. As the Yanks say. Now have you ever been out yourself for a night? It would be instructive. Oh yes. Such a night, it'd go on and on and on forever. You shiver, you ache, you turn one way, you turn the other, you go stiff as a board. You think you can sleep? Try it for a night. It's not on, and that's a fact. Dere's the cold and the wind, sure. But there's also that kind of feeling that you don't know who's going to creep up on you. Oh Mary, yes, you don't know till you're on the streets how many men t'ink they're the toughest. You get to wishing the cold would numb the thought out of your body. Your poor body! You wonder how it can stand so much distress. You just didn't know it was possible to be so miserable. Pains everywhere. Fears like lightning, crazy thoughts zigzagging through your tired old brainbox. Jesus! Try it for just one night. It'd be an adventure for you. You could boast about it afterwards, be a hero. That's all it'ld be for you, a fuckin' adventure. It's my fuckin' life...'

He shudders violently. 'Ah, pay no notice. It's the Prince of Denmark talking, "Alas poor Shorick I knew him well." No. I was telling you about this night, the coldest bejasus ever hurled at yours sincerely. It was down Mortimer Street, you'll have heard of that place? Ah, the Devil's soup kitchen that is. But, you have to realize, I'm a working man. I can't bear the not having work, its the reason I'll help anyone out around here. It's in the old blood. I'd been thrown out of the old family mansion, but t'ings didn't stop there. Three days I toured round the sites. I'm a good labourer, though I say so myself, but I'm known for it. Always willing. But it was the old Black Friar every single place. So I heard about this employment exchange for men like me, you know, no fixed abode. Mortimer Street. I went down there. Midnight, one o'clock, I'd got the wink to get there early. Fuck me, there's a queue already. Half a dozen men in cardboard boxes. If I tell you my luck was out, I'm lying through inexaggeration. Not a single piece of cardboard wadding to be found. And the night...! Four o'clock there's twenty or thirty of us. Five o'clock it's the council dustmen come to turf the Lucky Jims out of their boxes. Six o'clock and there's about sixty blokes, the lights go up inside. And then the doors are opened. Jesus Mary! Fighting! You've never seen the like. To talk about the jungle is doing the animals an injustice. And what for? I was told I was lucky. I got taken on casual at Harrods. Harrods! Portering. Lasted three days. And that was supposed to be the bee's knees of a cinch...'

The system has institutionalized the requirement for low-paid casual labour through Mortimer Street Employment Exchange which deals exclusively with this area of employment. When the pain and anguish of the men (often hostel-dwellers and dossers), as demonstrated graphically in their brawling for a single day's lousy work, attracted the attention of the media, the officials at the employment exchange changed the system. Before, men queued through the night. Afterwards they had to queue in the early evening. The first thirty or so would be given numbered cards. They would then have to bring these back at six the next morning when the jobs would be dispensed, as available, according to the number on their card. At first, this appears a better system; better, that is, for the men. But casual jobs often last for no more than a day and continue until the early evening. The effect of the new system ensures that it is almost impossible for someone who has been in work one day to be able to queue for work for the next day: he is still at his job. The system is not designed to help the men, but to ensure the least trouble possible. The fighting of the men for jobs was tolerated; the attention of the press was not. A change in the system was necessary – a change which could hide the existence of this desperation from the rest of society.

One morning we tried for a job as sandwich men. We went at five to an alley-way behind some offices, but there was already a queue of thirty or forty men waiting, and after two hours we were told that there was no work for us. We had not missed much, for sandwich men have an unenviable job. They are paid about three shillings a day for ten hours' work – it is hard work, especially in windy weather, and there is no skulking, for an inspector comes round frequently to see that the men are on their beat. To add to their troubles, they are only engaged by the day, or sometimes for three days, never weekly, so that they have to wait for hours for their job every morning. The number of unemployed men who are ready to do the work makes them powerless to fight for better treatment. The job all sandwich men covet is distributing handbills, which is paid for at the same rate. When you see a man distributing handbills you can do him a good turn by taking one, for he goes off duty when he has distributed all his bills . . .

. . . People are wrong when they think that an unemployed man only worries about losing his wages; on the contrary, an illiterate man, with the work habit in his bones, needs work even more than he needs money. An educated man can put up with enforced idleness, which is one of the worst evils of poverty. But a man like Paddy, with no means of filling up time, is as miserable out of work as a dog on the chain. That is why it is such nonsense to pretend that those who have 'come down in the world' are to be pitied above all others. The man who really merits pity is the man who has been down from the start, and faces poverty with a blank, resourceless mind.

Robert gets out of his squat on the Haygate Estate early and spends most days hanging around the West End and Piccadilly, sometimes on the streets, sometimes in the cafés, sometimes in the fruit machine arcades, sometimes in centres like New Horizon which have been set up to try and deal with the rising tide of homeless young people in London. 'Try' is the operative word: such centres are given as little money as possible to do their job which, at least in some quarters, has been redefined from solving the problem of youth homelessness to containing the youth and keeping them off the streets. It is cheaper to do this than to spend money on police, courts and prisons. Despite the limitations imposed on them, however, voluntary agencies like New Horizon represent one of the few important differences (and improvements) between Orwell's time and today.

Today Robert is hanging around with Jim, even though they don't like each other. Yet in some ways they are similar. Robert with his Army background is always dressed neatly; Jim carries tidiness to extremes. He has something of a fetish about cleanliness: 'Sometimes I wake up at night and sniff my armpits. If there's even a trace of a smell, I'm out of my bed and into the shower. You can't allow yourself to let yourself go.'

In other ways they differ markedly. Jim used to be active on the gay rent scene. 'Aye, you used to see me on what the papers called "the meat rack". The scene has moved on since then, up Wardour Street. I'm not so involved with that anymore. I mean, you can only be a male prostitute for just so long. Then the police start picking you up all the time. It gets too heavy.'

Robert rejects all this with scorn: 'You won't find me peddling my bumhole down Piccadilly. And I'm not going to start accepting dole or charity now. No, if I can't get a job, then I'll have to thieve. Not mugging, I can't stand mugging. But thieving. From shops and companies. They're the ones making us pay. Let them pay for a change.'

Robert and Jim are two of the homeless people who pass unnoticed. Though they sleep on a circuit of squats, friends' floors, voluntary agency hostels and occasional nights out rough, they are indistinguishable from any other twenty-three-year-olds.

On the corner of Great Queen Street and Drury Lane two pin-striped gentlemen with umbrellas unfurled against the continuous drizzle stop them and ask directions to Great Queen Street. With formal courtesy and great seriousness, they direct the gentlemen to a street beyond the British Museum. 'Fair game,' remarks Robert afterwards, before they go their different ways: he to the Job Centre ('Just in case I strike lucky'), Jim to look for other mates.

They are invisible. Another youth at New Horizon once said: 'I believe that there are other intelligent beings in the universe. In fact, some of them are here on earth. Only we can't tell them apart from us. They walk around and talk just like humans, like us. I don't know why they're here, whether it's to take us over or to guide us back onto the right path.'

There is a tradition of Hollywood horror movies based on the proposition that aliens – or zombies or robots – indistinguishable from humans are about to take over. The barbarians are taking over Rome; the lunatics taking over the asylum. The new homeless, the youth, are invisible; are they the vandals, muggers and brutalized yobbos we sometimes fear are threatening society?

There is a direct statistical correlation between unemployment and homelessness, and the phenomenon in society which makes sense of this is migration. Nevertheless, it is possible to conceive of a situation where there is large-scale unemployment and yet no homelessness. If the Welfare State was effective, then this ideal could be achieved.

Why, despite the Welfare State and the blossoming of numerous voluntary agencies within the past fifteen years, does this ideal seem further away than ever? The usual explanation is to state that there is a housing shortage in London. In one sense this statement is true. In another, it conceals. There are many empty houses in London. The housing shortage is a specific shortage of houses of specific types at specific rents.

The decline in private rented properties in London over the past quarter of a century has been dramatic. Today's empty properties are an obvious symbol of this decline. They are empty because it benefits the owner to leave them empty, in the hope of either selling or redeveloping them. Until recently property was one of the most profitable as well as one of the most secure investments. These days, though it remains secure, its profitability is inferior to a number of other forms of investment. For these reasons there has been a decline in private rented accommodation in London. The effect of this decline, despite laws to maintain 'fair' rents, has been to push rents upwards.

There has also been a shortage in the public rented sector. In recent years there has been little renewal of housing stock and this has combined with the faster than expected decay of fifties' and sixties' tower blocks. Many of these properties are now unlettable, while the better properties have been sold off cheap to the tenants; and the effect has been a drastic increase in the cost of repairs. In turn, rents have had to increase, or be massively subsidized, and rent arrears have mounted, leading to evictions.

Nevertheless, despite these specific shortages, it can be argued that homelessness is unnecessary, that the Welfare State should be able to overcome these deficiencies. And in some ways it does. It has continued the system of casual wards (dormitories for vagrants attached to workhouses) in its resettlement centres. It has instituted a maze of payments for rent, lodgings and bed and breakfast. (The regulations governing these have become so complicated that a number of voluntary agencies have grown up to help the individual to secure his rights.) Though the hotels in Earl's Court and other places are shabby and uncomfortable (and their owners profiteering), they are preferable to the spike or the Victorian institutions – the Salvation Army hostels and the Rowton Houses – which grew up as a response to the specific shortages of their day.

———————

At about a quarter to six the Irishman led me to the spike. It was a grim, smoky yellow cube of brick, standing in a corner of the workhouse grounds. With its rows of tiny barred windows, and a high wall and iron gates separating it from the road, it looked much like a prison. Already a long queue of ragged men had formed up, waiting for the gates to open. They were of all kinds and ages, the youngest a fresh-faced boy of sixteen, the oldest a doubled-up, toothless mummy of seventy-five. Some were hardened tramps, recognizable by their sticks and billies and dust-darkened faces; some were factory hands out of work, some agricultural labourers, one a clerk in a collar and tie, two certainly imbeciles. Seen in the mass, lounging there, they were a disgusting sight; nothing villainous or dangerous, but a graceless, mangy crew, nearly all ragged and palpably underfed. They were friendly, however, and asked no questions. Many offered me tobacco - cigarette ends, that is.

We leaned against the wall, smoking, and the tramps began to talk about the spikes they had been in recently. It appeared from what they said that all spikes are different, each with its peculiar merits and demerits, and it is important to know these when you are on the road. An old hand will tell you the peculiarities of every spike in England, as: at A you are allowed to smoke but there are bugs in the cells; at B the beds are comfortable but the porter is a bully; at C they let you out early in the morning but the tea is undrinkable; at D the officials steal your money if you have any – and so on interminably. There are regular beaten tracks where the spikes are within a day's march of one another. I was told that the Barnet–St Albans route is the best, and they warned me to steer clear of Billericay and Chelmsford, also Ide Hill in Kent. Chelsea was said to be the most luxurious spike in England; someone, praising it, said that the blankets there were more like prison than the spike. Tramps go far afield in summer, and in winter they circle as much as possible round the large towns, where it is warmer and there is more charity. But they have to keep moving, for you may not enter any one spike, or any two London spikes, more than once a month, on pain of being confined for a week.

---

He was told later that he had been lucky. He had turned up at Camberwell Resettlement Centre at around five o'clock. Within half an hour one of the porters had called him to the reception office. Sometimes, apparently, one has to wait hours. Sometimes there are fights. He was asked his name, his personal details, where he had slept the night before, then he was passed into the shower room and his clothes inspected for lice. After this his clothes were put into a cellophane bag and he was ordered to shower. The shower was freezing. Sometimes, apparently, it is so hot as to be unbearable. He was issued with overalls; then, when he had put them on, led back to the interview room for a second desultory examination. He was asked this time how much money he had.

He tells his story as though it is the story of someone else, some other forty-year-old man who has quarrelled with his wife, left home, kipped in a friend's council flat until told to move on, then been told by his local Brighton DHSS office that he wasn't eligible since he was of No Fixed Abode (NFA), but grudgingly given a travel warrant to London. This other person arrived in London and spent days and nights walking the streets, finding nowhere to rest. He tried one night under the arches in Charing Cross and gave that up as a bad deal. He tried one night in the Simon Community's night shelter in Camden Town. He hadn't liked it there, though the staff were friendly enough. But it was too rough, it stank, he had had to sleep on the floor sharing a room with four other men he'd only met that night. He slept rough for two nights, then slept in the Camden Emergency Night Shelter for three nights, the most he was allowed, even though it was worse than the Simon. He went to Bruce House one night. That was even worse; he couldn't believe how bad it was.

Tonight he is trying the spike and, despite the miserable wrinkled old man who shares the shower with him and tells him repeatedly how lucky he is, it is his worst experience yet.

He receives his bed ticket, goes to the dining room where he is given some gristly stew, some bread and hard cheese, and tea. He hardly notices that he is eating. A jolly, high-spirited, yet gentle drunk takes a liking to him and decides to show him the ropes. He leads him to the blanket room, and from there to his dormitory; even helps him make the bed and scrounges a clean pillow. After this, he takes himself off to the television room. At nine thirty, too tired for anything else, he goes back to his dormitory and falls asleep.

Half an hour later he is woken roughly. It is dark. There are shouts and curses from all around the dormitory. There is a fight going on in one corner, but he doesn't worry about that. He has been woken by someone trying to get into his bed. He lashes out feebly. Luckily, the intruder is worse off than he is and falls onto the floor where he lies gently moaning.

He stays awake for the next two hours. Gradually the shouts and curses die down, the sporadic fighting stops. The intruder ceases moaning, seems to slide further away under someone else's bunk. By this time, he needs to go to the toilet. He decides to risk it and leaves his bed.

He finds the toilets covered in ordure. The smell, the sight and his misery combine and he retches in a corner. For a second afterwards his brain clears and he regains courage. Tomorrow he will return home, make a pact with his wife, find work... Then the impossibility of the project defeats him. He smells his own sick among the competing smells of piss, shit, alcohol, stale sweat and cigarettes. He feels ashamed. He shuffles back to bed.

---

The scene in the bathroom was extraordinarily repulsive. Fifty dirty, stark-naked men elbowing each other in a room twenty feet square, with only two bathtubs and two slimy roller towels between them all. I shall never forget the reek of dirty feet. Less than half the tramps actually bathed (I heard them saying that hot water is 'weakening' to the system), but they all washed their faces and feet, and the horrid greasy little clouts known as toe-rags which they bind round their toes. Fresh water was only allowed for men who were having a complete bath, so many men had to bathe in water where others had washed their feet. The porter shoved us to and fro, giving the rough side of his tongue when anyone wasted time. When my turn came for the bath, I asked if I might swill out the tub, which was streaked with dirt, before using it. He answered simply, 'Shut yer — mouth, and get on with yer bath!' That set the social tone of the place, and I did not speak again.

When we had finished bathing, the porter tied our clothes in bundles and gave us workhouse shirts - grey cotton things of doubtful cleanliness, like abbreviated nightgowns. We were sent along to the cells at once, and presently the porter and the Tramp Major brought our supper across from the workhouse. Each man's ration was a half-pound wedge of bread smeared with margarine, and a pint of bitter sugarless cocoa in a tin billy. Sitting on the floor we wolfed this in five minutes, and at about seven o'clock the cell doors were locked on the outside, to remain locked till eight in the morning.

---

Perhaps, eventually, he fell asleep. He can't be sure. But suddenly he is wakened by the porters shouting and banging their keys on the beds. He notices one old grey man in a bed at the far corner taking his time about getting up. The porters rush across, seize the old-timer by his hair and ruthlessly manhandle him out of bed.

He gets up quickly and goes to the washroom. Fifty or sixty smelly decrepit bodies are heaving and shoving. The sinks are cracked and scummy, the water stone cold. There are no towels. He walks away without washing.

In the yard he hears a blackbird singing and remembers the time when he was a kid he used to spend looking for birds' eggs. He smiles to himself and tries to locate the bird which is singing so lustily. He sees for the first time the barbed wire at the top of the high perimeter wall.

The breakfast bell rings. He trudges wearily over towards the dining room where the other inmates are fighting round the door. A porter tells him to hurry up. Breakfast is porridge, bread and a pint of tea. He eats without thinking. The tea tastes bitter and ashy. He drinks it to the bottom and almost swallows a limp cigarette end someone must have thrown in the mug the night before. His stomach heaves but he controls himself.

The head porter shouts, barks out a list of names. His is one of the names. He is being called to have an interview with the welfare officer.

The welfare officer is sympathetic but listless. Long ago he gave up in the face of the enormity of his task. He is directed to Scarborough Street, where he will be able, along with the other NFAs, to claim his daily allowance. The welfare officer advises him to claim his allowance, then hitch back to Brighton. He hints that if this is too much for him, then he could always skip onto a train. He could pay later when he was in work again.

He had been told in Brighton that London was the place to go, that that was where all the jobs were. Now he was being told in London that he'd be far better off going back to Brighton. That, at least, was where his home was.

He realizes that looking as he does and having no home he has little chance of getting a decent job. Before his marriage broke down he was a navvy. He doesn't mind getting his hands dirty; he is proud that he can work long and hard hours at jobs others couldn't stand. He defines a decent job as a labouring job, but one with some security. He realizes that he has no chance of this in London, London is too big, he doesn't know the system, there's no one here to back him up.

Suddenly it comes to him. He has been sent to London to earn enough money to be able to return to Brighton. He realizes that the longer he stays in London the more hateful he will grow against his wife.

He feels a sudden surge of feeling towards Brighton. Not the Brighton of the Marina, the mews garages, the yachts and the luxury restaurants; but the Brighton of Queen's Park, of the old Black Rock pool now closed, of the church hall at the top of Islingwood Road which mysteriously burnt down and was rebuilt as flats. It's decaying but he feels affection for it. More affection than he could ever feel for London.

He decides to leave London, to go back, to return home. But first, like all the other inmates of the spike, he is allocated a task by the porters. Everyone has a task. Some sweep dormitories, some clean out toilets, others open windows and fold mattresses. In a land of unemployment, the work ethic still holds fast at the spike.

_____

At eight the porter came along the passage unlocking the doors and shouting 'All out!' The doors opened, letting out a stale, fetid stink. At once the passage was full of squalid, grey-shirted figures, each chamber-pot in hand, scrambling for the bathroom. It appeared that in the morning only one tub of water was allowed for the lot of us, and when I arrived twenty tramps had already washed their faces; I took one glance at the black scum floating on the water, and went unwashed. After this we were given a breakfast identical with the previous night's supper, our clothes were returned to us, and we were ordered out into the yard to work. The work was peeling potatoes for the pauper's dinner, but it was a mere formality, to keep us occupied until the doctor came to inspect us. Most of the tramps frankly idled. The doctor turned up at about ten o'clock and we were told to go back to our cells, strip and wait in the passage for the inspection.

Naked and shivering, we lined up in the passage. You cannot conceive what ruinous, degenerate curs we looked, standing there in the merciless morning light. A tramp's clothes are bad, but they conceal far worse things; to see him as he really is, unmitigated, you must see him naked. Flat feet, pot bellies, hollow chests, sagging muscles – every kind of physical rottenness was there. Nearly everyone was under-nourished, and some clearly diseased; two men were wearing trusses, and as for the old mummy-like creature of seventy-five, one wondered how he could possibly make his daily march. Looking at our faces, unshaven and creased from the sleepless night, you would have thought that all of us were recovering from a week on the drink.

The inspection was designed merely to detect smallpox, and took no notice of our general condition. A young medical student, smoking a cigarette, walked rapidly along the line glancing us up and down, and not inquiring whether any man was well or ill. When my cell companion stripped I saw that his chest was covered with a red rash, and, having spent the night a few inches away from him, I fell into a panic about smallpox. The doctor, however, examined the rash and said it was due merely to under-nourishment.

After the inspection we dressed and were sent into the yard, where the porter called our names over, gave us back any possessions we had left at the office, and distributed meal tickets. These were worth sixpence each, and were directed to coffee-shops on the route we had named the night before. It was interesting to see that quite a number of the tramps could not read, and had to apply to myself and other 'scholards' to decipher their tickets.

_____

The history of architecture is revealing about our attitudes to homelessness. The most common type of house in Britain is the terraced house, a form of housing which developed during the Georgian period and flourished during Victorian and Edwardian times. In the nineteenth century the gap between rich and poor was widening. But there were more steps, and at smaller intervals, on the social ladder. Divisions by pay replaced divisions by trade. This social hierarchy was reflected in an architectural hierarchy which was expressed not only in the size of the house and number of rooms, but in every particular down to the minutest item of decoration – even to the names of the streets, 'road' being considered superior to 'street'.

Each class and sub-class kept strictly to itself. The notion of a street as the shortest route between two points to be used by everyone could not be taken for granted. The most saleable element of a street was its class homogeneity. A change of class meant moving house, moving into another district.

There was one break in this architectural continuum – the break between the terraced house, no matter how mean and undecorated, and the hostel or workhouse. The architecture of the terraced house implied a community between the rich and the 'respectable poor'. This community did not extend to the hostel-dwellers and paupers, the 'undeserving poor'. Throughout the nineteenth century authorities charged with constructing workhouses and philanthropists seeking to aid the needy steadfastly ignored the model of the terrace. Instead they chose as their model the industrial dwelling, the barracks, the factory, the prison.

The hostel or workhouse, with its dormitories, its open staircases and its often badly fitting windows (to allow constant ventilation in order to blow the germs away – the Victorians had learnt early that infectious diseases do not respect class barriers), was justified on the grounds of cost and economies of scale. The history of homelessness has been a history of penny-pinching. Meanwhile, no attempt was made at decoration (until the Rowton Houses) because, in the words of one commentator of the time, it 'would frighten at the very entrance those whom the house was intended to benefit'. The history of homelessness has also been a history of apologetics, of excusing dire conditions and low standards on the grounds that the poor and the homeless would be put off by the everyday standards of comfort, shelter, hygiene and privacy that we expect as a matter of course.

Hostels and workhouses also act as a deterrent. They are potent reminders for the rest of the population of the fate that awaits those who become destitute. One of the central beliefs of the British form of capitalism is that the individual can be delivered from poverty by his own effort and enterprise. To be down and out is one's own fault. It is to stand guilty in the sight of the Lord.

Those attitudes (particularly with the recent propaganda favouring a return to 'Victorian values') are still with us today. So, too, are the hostels, which have a further disadvantage: their architecture to a large extent determines the way that the inmates will be treated. Only cosmetic changes can be made. For instance, the Salvation Army hostels, though the Salvation Army itself puts more emphasis on the 'whole man' and on using the social, medical and psychiatric facilities available through the Welfare State, remain much as Orwell described them.

At six we went to a Salvation Army shelter. We could not book beds till eight and it was not certain that there would be any vacant, but an official, who called us 'Brother', let us in on the condition that we paid for two cups of tea. The main hall of the shelter was a great, white-washed barn of a place, oppressively clean and bare, with no fires. Two hundred decentish, rather subdued-looking people were sitting packed on long wooden benches. One or two officers in uniform prowled up and down. On the wall were pictures of General Booth, and notices prohibiting cooking, drinking, spitting, swearing, quarrelling, and gambling...

To my eye these Salvation Army shelters, though clean, are far drearier than the worst of the common lodging-houses. There is such a hopelessness about some of the people there – decent, broken-down types who have pawned their collars but are still trying for office jobs. Coming to a Salvation Army shelter, where it is at least clean, is their last clutch at respectability...

The charge for beds was eightpence. Paddy and I had fivepence left, and we spent it at the 'bar', where food was cheap, though not so cheap as in some common lodging-houses. The tea appeared to be made with tea *dust*, which I fancy had been given to the Salvation Army in charity, though they sold it at threehalfpence a cup. It was foul stuff. At ten o'clock an officer marched round the hall blowing the whistle. Immediately everyone stood up.

'What's this for?' I said to Paddy, astonished.

'Dat means you has to go off to bed. An' you has to look sharp about it, too.'

Obediently as sheep, the whole two hundred men trooped off to bed, under the command of the officers.

The dormitory was a great attic like a barrack room, with sixty or seventy beds in it. They were clean and tolerably comfortable, but very narrow and very close together, so that one breathed straight into one's neighbour's face. Two officers slept in the room, to see that there was no smoking and no talking after lights-out. Paddy and I had scarcely a wink of sleep, for there was a man near us who had some nervous trouble, shellshock perhaps, which made him cry out 'Pip!' at irregular intervals. It was a loud, startling noise, something like the toot of a small motor-horn. You never knew when it was coming, and it was a sure preventer of sleep. It appeared that Pip, as the others called him, slept regularly in the shelter, and he must have kept ten or twenty people awake every night. He was an example of the kind of thing that prevents one from ever getting enough sleep when men are herded as they are in these lodging-houses.

At seven another whistle blew, and the officers went round shaking those who did not get up at once. Since then I have slept in a number of Salvation Army shelters, and found that though the different houses vary a little, this semi-military discipline is the same in all of them. They are certainly cheap, but they are too like workhouses for my taste. In some of them there is even a compulsory religious service once or twice a week, which the lodgers must attend or leave the house. The fact is that the Salvation Army are so in the habit of thinking themselves a charitable body that they cannot even run a lodging-house without making it stink of charity.

Hardly a day passes without Taff and his mate, Scouser, having a set-to. It's always the same argument. Today it blows up in the television room of

Arlington House. This is a long, dreary, stale-smelling room the size of a small cinema and filled with an odd jumble of sagging armchairs and rickety seats vaguely arranged in rows. Raised up at the far end a large black-and-white television blares, the sound distorted by volume and an uneasy echo.

It's an item about the Jarrow Hunger March which sets them off.

'I remember that,' Scouser says. 'I came in behind them. When they got to London, by God, the police got stuck in.'

'They were proper marches,' Taff agrees. 'They were proper fuckin' hungry. Now they march for shit.' Here his thought skips. 'If you're a single person you're shitted.'

'Right. We're classed as second-class citizens. Dossers.'

'I'm no fuckin' dosser!'

'Aye, we all know that fine,' a voice says from two rows in front. This is Mac, from Portobello in Edinburgh, a retired clerk who has lived in Arlington House for over twenty years. He still holds himself as stiff as a ramrod, still dresses immaculately in a dark-blue pin-striped three-piece suit, still polishes his shoes every morning until he can see his face in the toecaps. 'We all know that,' he says. 'And we're all heartily sick of it, Taff. This is the televison room and, believe it or not, some of us are here to watch television. So kindly continue your discussion elsewhere.'

There is mumbled agreement all round. Sulkily, Taff and Scouser troop out into the corridor. This is faced with glazed bricks similar to those in old tube stations. Richard Farrant, the architect, also advised on the construction of the Central London Tube and used many of the same techniques in his designs for the Rowton Houses. Dried-out yellowed paintings of steam trains and sailing ships – heralds to the era of enlightened progress – hang skew along the walls. They are one of the personal touches of Lord Rowton, whose motto was 'Philanthropy plus five per cent'.

A security guard lounges along the corridor, belches loudly, looks at them idly, then passes by. Further along he blows his nose between his fingers.

'Will you look at that!' Scouser says in disgust. 'The staff here are a shower. Even them security so-called guards. Them most of all. They're the same as us. Dossers. Since Rowton decided to sell out, things have gone from bad to worse.'

For years most of the staff of Arlington House had been selected from the lodgers. It was a convenient way of keeping wages low, since the room went with the job. It was, anyway, the traditional way of staffing hostels. Then, about eighteen months previously, the staff had organized themselves into a union. There was a strike for union recognition. After months of dispute, the management of Rowton Houses accepted defeat. Shortly after, the staff – now unionized – started negotiations for better wages and conditions. Their demands would have brought them near to the recognized minimum wage. Negotiations broke down and the staff, at the time of Taff and Scouser's discussion, had been on strike for some months. The management had brought in an outside firm of security guards to supplement the few lodgers who continued to work. Shortly afterwards, Camden Council began negotiations with Rowton Houses to buy Arlington House. (Similar moves were also afoot by the other local councils to buy the other London hostels of Rowton Houses.) Camden had been placed in an invidious position. They had either to buy Arlington House and then improve it at considerable cost so that it complied with fire and public health regulations; or they had to close Arlington House down and then immediately rehouse almost 1,000 single men, many of them old and retired, some of them needing medical care. They opted to buy Arlington House and plan, when it is bought, to halve the accommodation there by doubling the size of the bedrooms to seven foot by ten foot. During these negotiations, which have been dragging on for months, Rowton House management have stopped all repairs and put the rent of the seven feet by five feet cubicles up to around £17 per week.

Taff shakes his head. 'No, it's the men that make the place. You can't blame the management. Listen, if someone pisses or shits on my landing – now it's happened – who's to blame? If everyone thought of others it would be great, but they don't. Now, if someone slams his door, who's there to stop it? Instead, you've got fifty doors leading into fifty fuckin' little cells – I'm talking about my landing – and everybody's slamming their doors. It's a wonder the partitions don't crack. Plywood, that's all they are. It's the fuckin' people, Scouser, the people.'

'No, it's the environment. You walk in that front door and it puts twenty fuckin' years on you. Look at it, Taff. The canteen's been closed down on grounds of health. One side of the main toilets has been closed for months. "Temporarily for repairs"! And the jakes up the stairs are filthy. They're never cleaned. Look at this corridor – dog-ends, filth, snot. It's a TB trap, that's what it is.'

'Oh, you're getting like old—' Taff mentions the manager at another hostel who is obsessed by the knowledge that TB is on the increase among hostel-dwellers, and fears that he may catch it.

'And why not? It's a killer. See, we should have a sick bay here, permanent medical staff. Instead if anyone pisses their bed they're fined six quid. And they never get a new mattress. They get another pissed-on one. Remember that poor old bugger, retired chap, his giro didn't turn up one week. Slung out on the spot. You've got no security here. None. So what can you expect?'

'This place could be like a palace today and it would be like a shithouse tomorrow. You've got to go back to square one. That's the trouble with the world today, people are going backwards instead of forwards. What good does it do you?'

'That's what I'm saying. We're classed as second-class citizens.'

'I'm no fuckin' dosser. It's what I think of myself that matters.'

'No Fixed Abode.'

'You can vote.'

'First class is when you've got an address. Second class is when you live some place like this and have to go down to Scarborough Street. Now that's a filthy hole.'

'See, Scouser, I've never had no complaints. I'm scruffy. I go down the Mall often because I like to see the Changing of the Guard. I've never been picked up. I was down there when the Pope went to the Palace.'

'Well, I was picked up by the police. They had me spreadeagled. They went through me, up and down my legs.'

'Perhaps you were smiling at the men passing by,' Taff jokes.

'I was smiling at the horses. That's not the point. If the police don't like your face they pull you.'

'It's just circumstances. I had a nice steady job. I never thought I'd end up here. But I'm never classed as a dosser. I go to the Bingo and everyone is friendly. I'm a retired person.'

'Well, I had a nice steady job. In a wine bar in the city. It paid me fifty-three quid after deductions. I can get forty-nine quid with my Army pension and the social security. What's the point in working for four quid? Now, if it was even just a tenner, it'd be worth considering. You've got to work ...'

The conversation goes round and round. Eventually Scouser takes out his trump card.

'I went down to Oxford last year ...'

'I know, you ran away from me, that's what you did,' jokes Taff.

'I fancied a change. You know, I was there when it happened.' He pulls out newspaper clippings and a copy of Hansard from his pocket.

'You follow these things too closely,' counsels Taff.

'You weren't there. I was sent down. You can read it here. It's all in here. Facts, Taff, facts.' He waves the clippings, thumps the Hansard. 'That Cronin. The biggest bastard walking on two legs and he's still doing it today. He gives you a note for the nob. Seventy-five were supposed to be living in his two houses. We was all supposed to be on the fiddle. And we were sent down. But not Cronin, the guy on the top of the shit-heap. Not him. That's what I'm talking about. Second-class citizens.'

On 2 September 1982, 283 people who walked into an unemployment benefit office in Oxford found themselves arrested by the police on suspicion of fraud. The Thames Valley Police and the local DHSS had set up a fake 'temporary' office. They did this in order to catch people who had been giving false addresses in order to claim extra money.

Though a large number of the arrested were innocent, they were held throughout the day in boarded-up rooms, and denied the limited rights allowed to people under arrest. Later they appeared before special courts where they were denied access to solicitors before appearing in front of the magistrates. The great majority were held in custody until a later date.

Relatives, city councillors, probation officers and social workers were not told about who had been arrested, nor what would happen to them. Yet the media had been told beforehand. Press and television reported the story as a crime drama and seriously exaggerated the extent of the fraud. The police suggested links with organized crime. Yet the landlords at the centre of the affair, Cronin and Patel, escaped scot-free and, although picked up briefly for questioning, were allowed to continue their livelihood unimpeded by police investigations. They became principal witnesses for the prosecution, but their evidence in court was too unreliable to be of use.

In Cronin's statement to the Thames Valley Police he says that in his four houses he accommodates 'approximately seventy-five people'. At the time he charged £42 per week. Using this as a basis, his potential annual income is £163,800. Cronin, who owns a £100,000 house in Sunningwell, Berkshire, admitted annual profits of £28,000 on a £100,000 turnover. This is widely believed to be a conservative estimate.*

The attitude of the police towards dossers is also shown in an incident we saw in York Way by King's Cross at about nine o'clock one evening.

A large drinking school, including two women, are sitting on the pavement by the betting shop. They are having a rare time, passing the cider bottle. But though they are an unsightly mess and quite boisterously enjoying themselves, the pavement is wide, the pedestrians few. A white police transit van draws up and four or five young policemen tumble out and begin carting the loudly protesting members of the school into the van. The police are relaxed, almost merry. 'It's an offence, you know,' one explains. 'Besides, we're only helping a probationer out. He's got to make so many arrests, otherwise he's in trouble.' The last of the drinking school, a vociferous old woman, is complaining loudly and waving her arms in random defence as she is being lifted. 'Oh come on,' shouts the driver. 'Leave her be. We've got enough here already.' The police jump into the van and roar off with their booty. The old lady protests loudly to the empty air.

Not, of course, that the police are alone in their attitude of treating the wanderer abroad as a second-class citizen.

The West End Mission is a long, low building situated one hundred yards north of Covent Garden with its opera house, its chic shopping piazza, its new developments and soaring rents. Outside the rain weeps continuously. Inside, around a hundred dossers huddle on small wooden seats arranged in rows. Hymn-books are distributed from a cupboard on one side. Towards the opposite wall, behind the pianist, is a doorway which leads to where the tea will be brewed. The room is featureless. Apart from a lithograph of Christ with thorns, there is an almost complete lack of decoration. Otherwise the room resembles a school room, a primary

* Reproduced from *Poor Law* by Ros Franey (CHAR, Civil Liberties, 1983).

school room of the old sort where adults talked down to children on the pretext of educating them.

A terrible wet stench rises from the unwilling congregation. An industrial fan churns in the back wall, fighting a losing battle against the smell. But nothing can conceal the reek of holiness which pervades the mission. A drinking school at the back argue and joke amongst themselves, at one point almost coming to blows. The pianist sits behind his instrument and carefully avoids looking at any of the battered and decrepit men or the few swaddled, withdrawn women.

At the appointed hour the door is closed and locked. One must, it appears, be prompt if one wishes to be saved (or partake of the tea after the service). The service begins. It is badly and patronizingly conducted. The pianist can hardly play. The congregation hardly bother to sing along with the minister and his helpers, a clutch of sharp-nosed old ladies in tightly buttoned wool coats and prim hats. Now and then the drinking school burst into full-throated and raucous song, usually at a line which makes reference to being drenched in the blood of the saviour.

When it is time for the sermon, the minister peremptorily signs to a tramp at the back to turn off the extractor fan. The sermon, however, is to be delivered by a visiting evangelist who, like his colleague, disdains dog-collar or vestments. The visiting evangelist presses his pudgy fingers onto the desk that serves as a pulpit, looks up at a point level with the extractor fan and makes a curious cough in his throat. Then he begins: 'Brothers and sisters, I think if we were honest with ourselves we would say that the reason why most of us are here today visiting the Lord's house is for the tea and biscuits at the end. The Lord God in His infinite wisdom knows that, and as you sit in His mansion He judges you and finds you wanting. Repent! Let your souls be saved! Think not of your stomachs! For know that the Lord Jesus trod on this earth and went hungry and was tempted. His Father has likewise placed us upon this His earth so that we may be tried and tested. So that we may go hungry. He is testing you. At this moment and every moment. Better to leave tonight without your tea and biscuits that your soul may be saved, than to stay and gorge and remain a sinner ...'

He continues this tirade for almost half an hour. Most of it is thinly disguised insults and bullying. Now and then he verbally applauds the other evangelist, the clutch of old ladies, the pianist and himself. He ransacks the minor prophets for quotes full of blood and doom. Most of it is, frankly, nonsense and wouldn't be stood for in any self-respecting Methodist chapel. It is mediocre, fifth-rate stuff, delivered without notes, without any sense of rhetoric or phrasing and, seemingly, without any order or sequence of thought.

The sermon done, a final blood-drenched hymn disposed of, the fan is switched on and everybody sits expectantly waiting for the serious business of the evening to begin. Two or three trusties gather in the hymn-books, and the old ladies work their way round the congregation, one dispensing strong sugared tea from a plastic jug and another following up after with a plate of biscuits which she holds close to her chest and from which she dispenses one rich tea and one ginger nut to each person. One man, who has spent most of the prayers profitably winking at anyone looking in his direction, tries to grab two cups but is shooed away by a third old lady. The drinking school make a great play of smacking their lips and one of them launches into a eulogy on the goodness of ginger nuts, though to no effect: flattery, at least the flattery of dossers, gets you nowhere here.

There are, however, as many cups of tea as anyone wants and, provided you like it strong and sweet, a seemingly inexhaustible supply is ferried forth from the back room. The drinking school have soon downed two pints of it a man. But most of the rest, even though it is still raining outside, have already sloped off, with an abject, guilty look, anxious to be gone.

How much of philanthropy and social do-gooding is just a disguise? How much is it related to the power that it confers on the giver? And is it not just another way of treating the homeless as second-class citizens? When you're homeless, it seems, you lose the right not to be preached at.

---

Outside the church quite a hundred men were waiting, dirty types who had gathered from far and wide at the news of a free tea, like kites round a dead buffalo. Presently the doors opened and a clergyman and some girls shepherded us into a gallery at the top of the church. It was an evangelical church, gaunt and wilfully ugly, with texts about blood and fire blazoned on the walls, and a hymn-book containing twelve hundred and fifty-one hymns; reading some of the hymns, I concluded that the book would do as it stood for an anthology of bad verse. There was to be a service after the tea, and the regular congregation were sitting in the well of the church below. It was a week-day, and there were only a few dozen of them, mostly stringy old women who reminded one of boiling-fowls. We ranged ourselves in the gallery pews and were given our tea; it was a one-pound jam-jar of tea each, with six slices of bread and margarine. As soon as tea was over, a dozen tramps who had stationed themselves near the door bolted to avoid the service; the rest stayed, less from gratitude than lacking the cheek to go.

The organ let out a few preliminary hoots and the service began. And instantly, as though at a signal, the tramps began to misbehave in the most outrageous way. One would not have thought such scenes possible in a church. All round the gallery men lolled in their pews, laughed, chattered, leaned over and flicked pellets of bread among the congregation; I had to restrain the man next to me, more or less by force, from lighting a cigarette. The tramps treated the service as a purely comic spectacle. It was, indeed, a sufficiently ludicrous service – the kind where there are sudden yells of 'Hallelujah!' and endless extempore prayers – but their behaviour passed all bounds ...

The scene had interested me. It was so different from the ordinary demeanour of tramps – from the abject worm-like gratitude with which they normally accept charity. The explanation, of course, was that we outnumbered the congregation and so were not afraid of them. A man receiving charity practically always hates his benefactor – it is a fixed characteristic of human nature; and, when he has fifty or a hundred others to back him, he will show it.

———————

The first major vagrancy law was passed in England in 1349, one year after the Black Death had decimated the labour force. It was designed to ensure landowners a supply of labour at a price they could afford. Through the next two centuries the enclosure of common land, the dissolution of the monasteries, the Wars of the Roses and other factors contributed to the problem of vagrancy. In the mid sixteenth century the focus of the vagrancy statutes changed from regulating the movement of labourers to the control of felons. These new laws were specifically designed to protect the property of commercial travellers who were becoming increasingly important within society. The emphasis of this new legislation, reaffirmed in subsequent acts up to this century, was with the criminal, not the economic activities of vagrants.

The contemporary attitude to vagrancy has shifted once again. Increasingly, legislators and policy-makers have redefined vagrants in terms of disease and social inadequacy, perhaps in response to the Welfare State and the emergence of a new sub-class of doctors, social workers and other professionals who service it; perhaps because of a bias in the research methods of the statisticians which, by its nature, leads to a concentration on the personal 'defects' of the homeless.

Society's response to the vagrant is a confused reflection of this history. It handles him variously as an offender, as ill or undersocialized.

But though they treat vagrants within a social, medical or psychological framework (rather than a criminal framework), social workers and the officials of the Welfare State are as much agents of social control as the police. Many social workers realize this. They realize, also, that there is a gulf between the ideal of the Welfare State and the Welfare State in practice. The ethos of the Poor Law and the workhouse still dominates the thinking of those politicians and officials who operate the Welfare State, not as it was intended – to benefit everyone – but as a means for continuing the divide between 'us' and 'them'.

But to treat vagrants within a social and medical framework has the advantage, at least, of recognizing them as victims rather than criminals. As the recent murders in Muswell Hill highlight, vagrants are more often attacked than attackers. (An equally sinister slaughter in Hackney recently underlines this: an old man skippering in an underground car park beaten to death with a gas canister and the words 'National Front' scrawled on the walls in his blood.)

Dosser, vagrant, tramp, drifter, bum, hobo. Beggar, scrounger, parasite, sponger. The words we use when talking about the homeless are vessels full of emotional meaning and significance. Though we may sometimes pretend otherwise, none of them are pure descriptions of a category, a way of life. They stand as emotional ciphers, as a bar to thought, imagination and sympathy. They are words whose main function is to recognize the distance between speaker and object. They are words designed to increase that distance.

Man, uniquely among animals, has a terrible talent for remaining indifferent to the plight of others of his own species.

Outside Westminster Cathedral, five thirty in the afternoon. There has been a sudden bloody fight between two members of the drinking school who use the concrete square in front of the cathedral. A policeman is standing one vagrant against a car, holding a scarf around his neck as a tourniquet. The vagrant has been stabbed in the neck. Blood is smeared down his front, is beginning to clot in his navel. The vagrant has smeared some chemical over his face, potassium permanganate perhaps, to judge by the purple hue, as protection against the cold. This makes the scene even more grisly. I cross to a man who has seen the incident and ask what happened. He looks at me with evident distaste and says brusquely that he didn't see a thing. A woman dressed in tweeds asks me, 'Why are you so interested? Is it just curiosity?' I reply that I am a journalist who is interested in homelessness, that I was passing by. 'Oh, I suppose it was just too good to be true,' she answers venomously and darts back into the crowd of onlookers. The ambulance arrives. The tramp is led inside. Quickly the man and the woman emerge from the crowd and get into the Maxi on which the vagrant was leaning and drive off. Perhaps they are deciding, as a matter of priority, to visit the car wash.

We attempt to ignore vagrants. We shut them from our sight. We are blind to them. It is as though there is a conspiracy within society to ignore these people, a conspiracy which extends to our implicit agreement that the callous and inadequate methods which society employs for the rehabilitation of these people are both adequately humanitarian and sufficient for the scale of the problem.

That many wanderers abroad prefer to sleep out even in winter rather than enter the spike is not, as we may often suppose, a reflection on those sleeping rough, but on the government spike. It is not that they are out of their minds. It is rather that no one in their right mind would wish to stay in a spike unless absolutely pushed to it.

There is a twist to this conspiracy. We turn it into a contract with the vagrant population. We force them to recognize their isolation within society. We allow them to use public places as though they are their own private spaces. But we allow them to use only those public places which are sufficiently distant from the thoroughfares used by 'ordinary' people. For instance, 'cardboard city' under the arches at Charing Cross is on the south side of the road and to the west of the tube station – precisely the pavement which is the least used anyway. In republican France the streets are public property. Everyone recognizes that they are for the use of all. In Britain with our own ingrown and fixed idea and ideal of private property – voiced in such expressions as 'An Englishman's home is his castle' – public property is transmuted into the sphere of the private. We all use it, as it were, on sufferance. Public property does not belong to us, the people. It is as though it is the property of some quango situated between Whitehall and Buckingham Palace. Our ideal of private ownership and our idea of public property help to disfigure our already distorted attitude to the vagrant.

If the first rule of any society is to disguise the violence on which it is based, then our ideal of private property and our hypocrisy must be considered part of that disguise.

Many people view the system of segregation known as apartheid in South Africa with horror and loathing. Yet the system of segregation practised in this country, whereby the 'undeserving' poor are segregated from the rest of the population, goes virtually unremarked. They are tidied away into institutions – hostels, spikes, prisons. They have their own Social Security and employment offices. It is almost true to say that they have their own benches in the parks.

They have to put up with the worst jobs and the most unemployment. (It is a measure of the desperation of the homeless that they will work in appalling conditions for such low pay.)

Though it is difficult to remain clean if one sleeps rough, they are stigmatized for being dirty ('Cleanliness is next to Godliness'), in much the same way as the black people of South Africa are by the white population.

Their civil liberties are constantly ignored.

And our reactions are remarkably similar, even parallel, to those of the South African regime which constructs an ideology to justify its injustice: that the black race is inferior, less intelligent, inherently less law-abiding, incapable of government, etc. Similarly we construct an ideology to justify homelessness: that the homeless person is socially inadequate, alcoholic, criminal, etc.

It is an attitude which runs very deep.

---

... I had my dinner from the workhouse table, and it was a meal fit for a boa-constrictor – the largest meal I had eaten since my first day at the Hôtel X. The paupers said that they habitually gorged to the bursting-point on Sunday and were underfed the rest of the week. After dinner the cook set me to do the washing up, and told me to throw away the food that remained. The wastage was astonishing and, in the circumstances, appalling. Half-eaten joints of meat, and bucketfuls of broken bread and vegetables, were pitched away like so much rubbish and then defiled with tea-leaves. I filled five dustbins to overflowing with quite eatable food. And while I did so fifty tramps were sitting in the spike with their bellies half filled by the spike dinner of bread and cheese, and perhaps two cold boiled potatoes each in honour of Sunday. According to the paupers, the food was thrown away from deliberate policy, rather than that it should be given to the tramps.

At three I went back to the spike. The tramps had been sitting there since eight, with hardly room to move an elbow, and they were now half mad with boredom. Even smoking was at an end, for a tramp's tobacco is picked-up cigarette ends, and he starves if he is more than a few hours away from the pavement. Most of the men were too bored to talk; they just sat packed on the benches, staring at nothing, their scrubby faces split in two by enormous yawns. The room stank of *ennui*.

Paddy, his backside aching from the hard bench, was in a whimpering mood, and to pass the time away I talked with a rather superior tramp, a young carpenter who wore a collar and tie and was on the road, he said, for lack of a set of tools. He kept a little aloof from the other tramps, and held himself more like a free man than a casual. He had literary tastes, too, and carried a copy of *Quentin Durward* in his pocket. He told me that he never went into a spike unless driven there by hunger, sleeping under hedges and behind ricks in preference. Along the south coast he had begged by day and slept in bathing-huts for weeks at a time.

We talked of life on the road. He criticized the system that makes a tramp spend fourteen hours a day in the spike, and the other ten in walking and dodging the police. He spoke of his own case – six months at the public charge for want of a few pounds' worth of tools. It was idiotic, he said.

Then I told him about the wastage of food in the workhouse kitchen, and what I thought of it. And at that he changed his tone instantly. I saw that I had awakened the pew-renter who sleeps in every English workman. Though he had been famished along with the others, he at once saw reasons why the food should have been thrown away rather than given to the tramps. He admonished me quite severely.

'They have to do it,' he said. 'If they made these places too comfortable, you'd have all the scum of the country flocking into them. It's only the bad food as keeps all that scum away. These here tramps are too lazy to work, that's all that's wrong with them. You don't want to go encouraging of them. They're scum.'

I produced arguments to prove him wrong, but he would not listen. He kept repeating:

'You don't want to have any pity on these here tramps – scum, they are. You don't want to judge them by the same standards as men like you and me. They're scum, just scum.'

---

And so we continue with certain meaningless distinctions. For instance, the distinction between the 'deserving' and the 'undeserving' poor. And we continue to believe that different standards of shelter, comfort, hygiene and privacy should apply to the homeless.

We continue to foster the attitude that underlies the Poor Law and the workhouse: that while it is incumbent on the individual to find work even if that entails leaving home, it is only incumbent on the State to support the individual if he remains at home. (And then only in a punitive manner designed as a way of terrorizing the rest of the population.) How different is this to the attitude of the London local authorities, who will use any device to deny their responsibility for the single homeless in their area?

Given the way we treat the homeless, particularly the single homeless, why should we be surprised that they show a higher-than-average incidence of alcoholism, mental illness and venereal disease? But these are not the cause of the problem. They are (for a minority) the effects, and effects made more obvious because of their poverty and homelessness. (Wealth hides a multitude of sins: converts alcoholism into 'a drinking problem', mental illness into 'eccentricity'. What in the rich is forgivable becomes unacceptable in this minority of the single homeless.) They are symptoms of the intense spiritual agony of the homeless. They are an attempt to assuage the sense of loss of place, of job and of function. They are a response to the way society treats them. And they are part of a survival strategy.

The room achieves a state of mess and untidiness, yet has few of the usual props. There are none of the personal knick-knacks, pot-plants, magazines and newspapers, pieces of occasional furniture, pictures, books, decorations, records, lamps, scatter cushions, piles of discarded clothes that seem to accumulate in most homes.

The room achieves this mess because it acts as bedroom, living room and kitchen, and because four people live here. It has been designed – if the shoddy, careless conversion can be termed a design – as a bedsit for one couple; but at £70 per week for rent, Harry and Joyce have been forced to get others in to help pay the rent. Flight and Snowhite sleep on a cushion on the floor and contribute to the household economy.

The room's mess is a mess of dust, dirty cracked crockery, empty cigarette packets, noisy cheap carpet. The lagged hot-water boiler, the exposed pipes, the black-and-white television braying half-ignored to one side, the damp, faded wallpaper peeling up from the skirting boards – all these add to the confusion and dinginess.

The sun angles in through the dirty basement window. Outside, water from an overflow drips onto the narrow concrete area, green with lichen. A tube train rattles past the bottom of the wilderness which passes for a garden.

Harry places two brown pills on a dessertspoon, adds a little water and a drop of juice from a plastic lemon. Then, positioning the spoon over the edge of the table and pinning it down with a tumbler of water, he heats the spoon with two matches. Replacing the spoon on the table he mashes up its contents with the end of a matchstick. His actions are heavy with ritual.

Flight has brought over his strongbox and produced two plastic one-shot disposable needles. Harry cleans one by sucking in some water from the tumbler then pushing the syringe back. A tiny fountain of water curves across the room. He repeats this process four times, then nestles the needle into the solution in the spoon.

The others continue chatting and smoking. Henry has suddenly become interested in the film on television, an old American World War Two propaganda churn-out called *Confessions of a Nazi Spy*. Snowhite is putting her jeans on. Alison has slipped into the corner partitioned off as a bathroom.

There is momentary confusion. Flight isn't sure that the smack is strong enough, he thinks Harry has sucked up all the lemon and none of the heroin into the needle. He pulls at the tuft of his Mohican hairstyle. Harry tastes some of the solution on his fingertip and is satisfied.

He ties a tie tightly around his upper arm, flexes his arm to bring the veins to the surface. Then he fixes.

The fix completed he returns to bed, burying himself under the piled blankets.

Flight fixes using a leg-warmer as a tourniquet.

Alison returns from the bathroom where she has had a fix.

Flight starts fussing around his and Snowhite's bed, converting it into a makeshift couch. Snowhite prepares her fix.

Harry gets out of bed, switches channels on the television, gets back into bed.

Snowhite ties the leg-warmer around her arm, pulls it tight with her teeth.

Harry gets out of bed, switches channels on the television, spreads marge on a slice of Sunblest, gets back into bed.

Snowhite misses the vein and starts to panic. She calls for Flight's help. Flight is the expert, the high priest of heroin, the addict. 'It's dribbling,' she cries. 'Turn the barrel,' he counsels. 'Oh God, there's a blood clot!' Snowhite screams in a high, tinny voice. 'Don't worry,' Flight soothes, attending to her.

Blood mingles with the gear in the syringe. Flight takes it out, examines it, cleans it out. He replaces the needles in his strongbox.

'I'm not hit,' squeals Snowhite. 'Let's look at you,' murmurs Alison comfortably. 'Yeah, you're pinned.'

Harry gets out of bed, switches channels, gets back into bed. 'I want to see the film,' Henry says irritably. Motorbikes race across the screen in a whirlwind of distortion. 'Nah, sport,' mutters Harry. He gets up and fiddles with the aerial. The whirlwind on-screen continues. 'Fucking television,' he says getting back into bed.

'I've a bad habit,' Flight says, matter-of-fact. What's it like? 'Do you want some?' he offers.

'It's wonderful,' Alison replies, her face broad and placid. 'It's like on smack you feel totally together. Nothing can phase you. Only trouble is you itch.'

'It's the smack trying to get out of your system,' Flight explains.

Harry gets out of bed, switches channels, busies himself frying two eggs. Flight empties ashtrays. Henry settles back into the film. Alison gets up to go to the toilet. 'I don't know why it is, but I always puke up,' she says.

'Up West,' Flight expounds, 'it's getting harder and harder to score dope, but smack is getting easier. The street price is around ninety pounds for a gram, but I can get it for around fifty or seventy pounds. The difficulty is syringes. There used to be a place down Fulham, but now you have to go up Shaftesbury Avenue.'

Harry, back in bed, suggests a place up in Kilburn and proceeds to give long complicated directions to Snowhite who says she's going out later to try and buy some more needles. 'These are so blunt,' she wails, 'It's like sticking a rusty old drill into your arm.' But Harry's directions get too complicated and her attention wanders.

Why don't the police close down those chemists who sell syringes? Flight shrugs, 'It keeps disease down.'

Flight and Snowhite move back to their cushion and begin embracing passionately. They are happy, smiling, tender; more interested in each other's lips and bodies than in Edward G. Robinson who is belligerently unmasking a German spy-ring on the television.

Later, as they are leaving, Harry mumbles to Flight and Snowhite, 'Listen, I'm sorry about what happened last night.'

'We don't mind,' Snowhite replies briskly. 'It doesn't make any difference to us. It's Joyce you should think about, always bawling at her. You're hurting her.'

Outside, Snowhite says, 'He's fucking her up rotten.' She looks like a little Barbie doll in her black plastic mac and dyed black hair. She enjoys playing up to the image.

'Joyce just lets him. She just takes it all,' adds Flight.

Later Alison explains what it's all about. 'It's Flight and Snowhite's fault really,' she says. 'Harry and Joyce can't afford that place. So they got Flight and Snowhite in. It was only supposed to be for a fortnight. Flight and Snowhite had got chucked out of their last place. They were looking for somewhere. So they agreed a fortnight and said they'd help out with the rent. That was five weeks ago and all Flight gives is like the occasional fix. They just sponge off you. They're like that. They're always scrounging off you. Half the time I'm out looking for punters, I'm doing it for them and my other so-called friends, not for myself. I don't know why I do it.'

In the nineteenth century, administrative costs involved in running the colonial empires of Britain and France were largely financed by the opium trade. The smooth operation of the British Empire was underwritten by the wholesale addiction of the Chinese people. In the twentieth century, history has reversed this flow. In order to help win the Second World War, the United States government made certain concessions to the Mafia. In return, the troop landings in Sicily were secured. And in the Far East, first the French and then the Americans financed the opium-growing hill tribes of South East Asia in their efforts to deny communism victory in Vietnam.

At first the opium trade was directed to Saigon and to the American troops stationed there. With the American withdrawal and the discipline of communist rule, the drug traffic was diverted to the West. Production of opium in the Golden Triangle of South East Asia which for decades had remained relatively stable suddenly boomed. Opium became a cash crop for export. Today opium in the form of heroin is being exported to the West.

Heroin is a suppressant of nervous-system activity including reflex functions like coughing, respiration, heart rate and bowel activity. It can produce euphoria and distance from pain. Vomiting is usual for beginners. Long-term use leads to constipation, lack of appetite, reduced sex drive, interruption of the menstrual cycle. Tolerance develops. Withdrawal means sleeplessness, vomiting, cold sweats, stomach cramps. Depression usually lasts for months. Other serious problems relate to adulteration of heroin and injection of heroin. Adulteration can lead to poisoning and overdose. Injection can lead to collapsed veins, respiratory disease, malnutrition and hepatitis. Resistance to other disease is lowered.

It would be a mistake, however, to see heroin as 'the problem' and enshroud the drug in mystery. Homelessness is the problem. Given money, clean needles or sterilizing equipment can always be purchased: hepatitis is found on the streets, not in the comfortable houses of wealthy users. Given a home, a warm bed, a bath, the support of friends, it is far from impossible to kick the habit.

It is early Monday evening in a saloon bar in Whitechapel. Sam, fifty-nine, unemployed for three years, marriage broken, sits over his pint of Guinness. 'Ah, you've caught me in a meditative mood. Monday evening. Always the best time to talk to me.' He laughs shortly, without pleasure, and explains. 'Thursday is giro day and from lunch on Thursday till closing time on Sunday I'm drunk. Legless. Monday, the money is running out. I have to pace Monday. A pint at lunchtime, a meal in the afternoon along at the café – it's easy to forget about meals – and then a couple of pints in the evening. Remember to buy a half-ounce of tobacco. Then Tuesday and Wednesday I'm miserable as sin. Shaking. Can't go anywhere. If it rains, it rains on my head. If it's very bad I go to the library, but they don't like you in there. I'm conscious of their eyes, eyes full of hate.' He pauses for a drink, curls his tongue round his lips, licking off the foam. 'It's important to have a strategy, see. I could spend the money in the off-licence and stay drunk all week. I've worked it out. Economically, I could do it. But I need the pub, I need the human companionship. Where else could I get that? I've been all round the circuit. I've been in all the hostels, the Sally Army – terrible place – Bruce House, the spike one time. I've waited for all the soup-runs, down at the Embankment for the Silver Lady, over at Charing Cross or at Lincoln's Inn Fields for St Mungo and Simon Community and the Sally Army. I've queued up at Mortimer Street hoping for a job at something. I've waited at the DHSS place at Scarborough Street. You don't see nobody but yourself at all those places. You're cut off from society. At least, that is what I think. I've got to get out of that sometimes, pretend I'm normal. Human companionship. And it's got to be a pub because without the alcohol I couldn't face the way I'm living now, the things I have to put up with – being kept waiting for no good reason, being given a cup of tea by someone who thinks he's oh so superior, being forced to obey all their petty regulations at the hostel. I wouldn't mind if I could see any good reason behind them, but no one ever takes the time to explain. Well, people don't feel they have to explain anything to dogs, children or dossers ... Circles and circles. That's what life is. A series of revolving doors. Unemployment, drinking, the spike, the Sally Army, skippering out, pulled in by the police, prison, out again, no chance of a job, so drinking, the spike ... Thank goodness I haven't gone that far down. I haven't been to prison. I can't guarantee I won't, though. Once you fall below a certain line, it's very hard to get above it again. It's as though it's a parapet, I'm just clutching at the top with the tips of my fingers and some great sod comes and stomps his feet down on my fingers and I lose grip. The toughest part is knowing that most of the time the sods don't even realize what they're doing to you. They don't, you know. It's strange. I can't explain it. Fifty per cent of the time, they're hypersensitive to you, they hate you, loathe you, despise you. And the other fifty per cent of the time, it's as though you don't exist ...'

One of the enduring problems with homelessness is that so often a past solution to the problem of homelessness later becomes part of the problem itself. At one time, and in their own way, the government spike, the Salvation Army hostels and Rowton Houses were aimed at solving – or, at any rate, making better – homelessness. They were specific responses to specific housing shortages and specific influxes of people into London. There is little doubt that, say, Arlington House in its early years answered a need better than anything that preceded it. There is little doubt also that it answered the need better fifty or eighty years ago than it does now.

What, then, is to be done? The first step is to ask the homeless themselves what they want. This has been done, though no action has been taken on it, and all the studies show that the great majority of homeless people have realistic aspirations about the type of housing they require. Those who require supportive accommodation would like that form of accommodation. Those in need of sheltered housing indicate that they would prefer sheltered housing. Yet the majority are ordinary people and they ask only for ordinary decent housing.

Above Chummie's door there is a runic scrawl. This lets Chummie know which people entering his room are filled with evil intentions towards him. Chummie believes in superstition.

'Heroin? It's death, man,' he says emphatically. 'And I should know. I was a junkie. But I was one of the lucky ones, I kicked the habit. Prison was the worst time. Cold turkey. I suppose by the time I was sent down, I'd stuck as many needles in myself as in the animals down at the lab. But cold turkey!'

He shudders and shakes his head, unable to express the horrors of withdrawal. 'I suppose you could say I've fucked others over and I've fucked myself over and I'm still here. Not much left to do, is there?'

He finishes carefully rolling a joint and lights it. 'I hate Earl's Court. I don't go out any more in the day. I can't walk down the street without being picked up by the police. It's always either the drug squad or the burglary squad. I've been stitched up. They planted this screwdriver on me and claimed it was an offensive weapon.'

He watches the television for a time. 'What I want,' he resumes, 'is for me and Tim here to get a flat up somewhere like Holland Park. Just somewhere I can be anonymous.'

Shaun finishes the can of Special Brew and looks over at Peter. He whispers, 'The lad is in a terrible state. I'm thinking, if he's just a little better in the morning, I'm going to get him out of here. If I can just get him over that breezeblock wall out there. Maybe I'll knock it down, sure it would fall with just a couple of blows from the old sledgehammer. That's what I'll do, I'll knock it down. We won't be needing to come back here anyway. Then I'll get the pair of us over to a de-tox unit, they have a place down Marylebone. Surely they'll take us in? Ah, Jesus, they have to take Peter in, that's the main thing ... It's the old chicken and egg story. Which comes first – the drinking or the homelessness? It doesn't matter how you answer that old conundrum. The point is to kick one or the other. Now, what odds will you give me? What odds on the Irish black horse kicking the bottle? ... It's the only thing, that's for sure.'

The discipline that Robert learned with the Army stays with him. He enforces strict house rules on whoever is living with him at the squat. (The other inhabitants change frequently, perhaps because he is so strict.) He doesn't allow noise, mess or fighting. He is pointedly courteous to the other residents on his floor, most of whom are old-age pensioners for whom he feels a genuine respect. 'They fought in the war. They deserve everything we can give them, more than they're getting.'

Robert's unemployment and subsequent homelessness led him to re-examine himself, the world and his priorities. 'I realized that homelessness is something that happens to people, ordinary people. There's nothing inadequate about me. I'm not mentally disturbed, though sometimes with the insecurity of this life I'm amazed.' He joined CHAR, the Campaign for Single Homeless People, and is an active volunteer. Before, he found difficulty in reading or writing. Now, though he still has to follow the words with his finger, he's an avid reader – of newspaper reports, Hansard, government speeches, local council minutes, pamphlets. He is at home with all the controversies to do with homelessness.

Despite this, he frets about his unemployment. 'I don't want any money to keep me unemployed. I want money to work. I don't want to be sitting on me bollocks. They've got to start giving the money to councils rather than to the private landlords to line their own pockets. What's happened is everyone has come out of the war and thought, "This is paradise." Only later, they've been slapped with poverty again.'

It's turned cold again and the wind that comes off the Thames is raw and piercing. Now and then it throws a few drops of rain over the sooty plants and statues in Temple Gardens. An uneven, ragged line of almost a hundred men winds from the iron railings by the east entrance along the path to the stark circle of tarmac and wooden benches in the centre of the gardens. In summer, secretaries from the finance houses which line the northern side of the gardens eat their sandwiches and salads here. But today, the park is filled with vagrants and hostel-dwellers waiting for the arrival of the grey Silver Lady van which will dispense teas and pies to them. They hunch their shoulders, rub their hands or bury them deeper in their pockets. There are all sorts here: old, young, vagrants, hostel-dwellers, casual labourers, middle-aged men you would never dream were down and out. There are even one or two women.

Taff and Scouser are there, in the queue, arguing. Scouser is apologizing. 'It's not my fault, Taff. I ask them not to give me a giro for two weeks at a time. . .'

'There's too many of these handouts, Scouser, that's what it is.'

'I've never been good with money. I've always spent it.'

Taff shakes his head. 'It's getting to everybody these days. Take women today. I've got a niece, she has four kids. I've never seen her pick up a needle. She lives off Social Security and she's not badly off. Now when I look back on my old lady's life I feel sad. She had three miners, they all had to have a bath every night and there wasn't any electric. It was a tin bath in front of the fire. In the evening she was darning and sewing. In the morning she was up at four thirty to get us miners down the pit.'

For Taff, the world is not the same as it once was. And it is the people who are at fault. He looks at the queue, which is slowly moving forward towards the Silver Lady van. Men walk back singly or in pairs with pies with bites out of them in their hands and clutching cups of tea. 'Nothing much has changed, you know. Not in one way. They've changed a few things. Like the partitions in Arlington have been built up to the ceiling. And they've closed most of the spikes so you can't walk from one to the next no more. But it's the people that have changed.'

They take their teas and pies and walk through the gardens. For Taff and Scouser the future is of little concern. Their future lies in the past, in their memories. 'They'd only stop the coal if someone was killed. I've known times they'd keep the men in the pit by saying – if there was an accident, like – that it was only a broken leg. After eight hours on the coalface, you'd come up to the surface to find one of your buddies gone. Terrible, it was. You had everything against you. There was no sympathy in them days. Oh, but the feeling you had inside you. You don't find that any more.'

And yet, though the memories are mostly grim, it is to those he keeps returning. Memories of work. 'I remember one of the horses, he wouldn't move. You had stables down in the pit where the ground had settled. It was all whitewashed. There was this one horse wouldn't move unless you gave him a little bit of grass. Then he'd work all day. I loved that horse. Came the day for his retirement and he was taken up to the surface. You should have seen him in those fields. He was running about, fucking kicking he was, wild with joy. It must have felt great to be out in those fields.'

Scouser nods in agreement. 'The good old days. When people talk about the good old days, I smile because it must have been before my day.'

Five minutes after the Silver Lady van has driven away with a smoky rattle, the gardens are deserted. One hundred men have vanished again, into the streets and alleys and passages of London.

One member of the drinking school by Victoria Station is unlike the others. He is dressed respectably. He is not even a hostel-dweller, whose clothes, though often presentable and sometimes only barely out of fashion, are usually inappropriate, faintly absurd, ill-fitting. Not so this man. He is dressed in a smart navy-blue blazer, C & A trousers with a sharp crease, and unscuffed suède shoes. He has a rainbow badge in his lapel.

Yet his face is lined and battered and the skin has that raw look which comes from being out in the open. His fingers hold his cigarette loosely and the ash tumbles over his trousers. He has the unfocused stare of the drunk. And he is sitting among the drinking school as though he is among his own kind.

'Maybe Alcoholics Anonymous helps some people. It's no good as far as I'm concerned, it didn't help me ... You've got to go down. And when I say down, I mean *down*. Down till you touch bottom. I was a dosser. I'm thirteen, fourteen stone so you'll know what I mean when I tell you I was six stone. I was on the trains, going backwards and forwards. Sleeping rough. And I was on this train to Dover. I woke up and I realized I couldn't move. I couldn't get out of there. I couldn't jump the train. I just couldn't. No strength.' He gestures feebly. 'We were coming into Dover, I could see the tracks below me, the drop was only about twelve feet. And I thought, the only way off is just to roll ... So, I ... And I thought, Jesus Christ, is this it? ... And I rolled off ...

'I got up, began walking up the tracks. I almost got knocked over by a train going the other way. And I thought, "What am I doing here? I used to have a motorcar, a house. What's it all for?" I thought, "I've got to get a job."

'I got back and I went round to the Job Centre, just round the corner from here, and I said, "I want a job." And he got me an interview, he knew I was serious. He got me an interview for 6.35 that night. It was 5.30 . . .

'The trouble was, I met a mate and we went on the drink. The next day I woke up and I thought, "What have I done?" I'd turned down a good job, well, I hadn't got it, but I was in with a good chance, I knew it. So I rang up the firm and explained, they knew all about me and they told me to come round for an interview that day . . . And I didn't turn up. No, not even the second time . . .'

He pauses for a long time. The wind blows scraps of paper around his ankles, greasy packaging from a nearby Wimpy. His cigarette has burnt down to the filter and gone out. His concentration has lapsed but he retains sufficient presence of mind to make it appear as though he is considering matters carefully. Two vagrants stagger out from a nearby off-licence, one with his foot in a leather pouch, one with a vodka bottle. Automatically he stretches into his pocket, then hands round the Marlboros. It is the gesture of a friend who has struck lucky.

'I went to see some people I knew in Edgware and I said, "Give me a job." And they said, "Come off it, John." And I said, "No, I'm serious this time." They laughed. "You always say that." So I said, "Just let me work here like anyone else. Only you don't have to pay me. Don't pay me. Just let me work." And they said, "Well, we can't argue with that . . ." So I started working and now I've got a home and a wife. I'd been married before I hit the streets. Married and divorced. Now I'm married a second time.'

What is there in this way of life that he misses so much that he has to revisit it? What kind of companionship, what intense loyalty does he find here that he cannot discover in the society of the house?

It is Thursday night, giro night, in The Boltons. It feels as though half the youth who live in Earl's Court's shabby bed-and-breakfast land have been decanted into the packed pub. The fruit machine whirrs, the jukebox blasts away, the space invaders honk, the cash-till behind the counter rings constantly in furious response to the shouts and drinking. Despite the carpet and soft furnishings, the atmosphere is brittle and frenetic. Everyone seems self-dramatizing. A scuffle breaks out in a corner, though it is still early. Chairs are knocked over and drinks spilled. Then, as suddenly as it flared up, the fight dies down. Hanging on to each other, the two erstwhile contestants approach the bar and order another round of drinks.

Alison sips at her coke, Audrey at her gin and orange. Their eyes are blurred from heroin. Ian, a black youth with wet-look hair, who introduces himself as 'a part-time hairdresser and a full-time gay', is recounting his latest brush with the police. 'Then I was taken down to Kensington Police Station. Oh, they're so butch there; I could really get into body searches. There was one constable, oh my dears, he was so sweet and innocent. Pretending to be gruff and hard-man, you know, and his voice was still breaking. "Have you been done yet?" he asks. "Ooo, officer," I reply, sweetness and light, "I've been done five times already, but for you I'll be done again." And I reached for his hand, friendly like. You should have seen him. He turned red as a beetroot. I think, secretly, deep down, he fancied me.'

Alison and Audrey laugh. They enjoy the company of gay men, perhaps because they don't feel threatened by them.

'Everybody imagines that gays will bite you. But they're just like you and me,' Alison says.

'I could spend my life in this pub,' Audrey mumbles dreamily.

'You'd have to go out sometimes to score. And to pull a punter.'

'Yeah,' Audrey sniggers. 'You couldn't do either of them activities in the loo.'

Alison laughs and points to a jaded woman sitting on a bar stool alone by the counter. She has a headsquare over heavily lacquered hair and deep lines running down her face, which is caked with make-up. She wears stiletto heels and stockings with seams. 'That's Dorothy,' Alison explains. 'She's on the game. Some of the men she goes with are revolting. And you know how much she gets? A packet of cigarettes and a bag of chips.'

Dorothy gets down from her bar stool and goes into the ladies. 'That's where she washes,' Audrey whispers.

'It's terrible,' recounts Alison. 'At Christmas one of the gays here gave her a little chocolate egg as a present and she burst into tears. She'd never been given a present before.'

Dorothy comes out of the ladies. Her face is set and determined. She is willing herself, against all the fear and misery and physical disgust, to go out to work. She exits. Alison and Audrey follow her with their eyes. They look at her with pity and compassion, but seemingly with no consciousness that perhaps they might one day be reduced to her state.

'No, I want to be a social worker,' Alison states firmly. 'I've wanted to be one for ages. I reckon I'd be good at it. I mean, I've been through everything myself, so I know what to say and do. I've got an interview tomorrow with a community group, working with kids. I'd like that.'

'Hey, look, there's Snowhite. She doesn't usually come in here.'

'I wonder what she wants.'

Snowhite, looking pale, comes over and whispers to them urgently. Alison goes to the bar and buys her a drink, while Audrey consoles Snowhite. Later, Alison says as though casually, 'There was a bit of an accident, Snowhite's not quite sure what. She thinks maybe Harry took an overdose; they had to rush him to hospital in an ambulance. She doesn't know what to do. Flight's away and she doesn't want to go back to the flat. I said we'd all go back to our room. It's a bit too noisy in here ...' She departs with her arm round Snowhite, holding her protectively.

---

... Why do tramps exist at all? It is a curious thing, but very few people know what makes a tramp take to the road. And, because of the belief in the tramp-monster, the most fantastic reasons are suggested. It is said, for instance, that tramps tramp to avoid work, to beg more easily, to seek opportunities for crime, even – least probable of reasons – because they like tramping. I have even read in a book of criminology that the tramp is an atavism, a throw-back to the nomadic stage of humanity. And meanwhile the quite obvious cause of vagrancy is staring one in the face. Of course a tramp is not a nomadic atavism – one might as well say that a commercial traveller is an atavism. A tramp tramps, not because he likes it, but for the same reason as a car keeps to the left; because there happens to be a law compelling him to do so. A destitute man, if he is not supported by the parish, can only get relief at the casual wards, and as each casual ward will only admit him for one night, he is automatically kept moving. He is a vagrant because, in the state of the law, it is that or starve. But people have been brought up to believe in the tramp-monster, and so they prefer to think that there must be some more or less villainous motive for tramping.

As a matter of fact, very little of the tramp-monster will survive inquiry. Take the generally accepted idea that tramps are dangerous characters. Quite apart from experience, one can say *a priori* that very few tramps are dangerous, because if they were dangerous they would be treated accordingly. A casual ward will often admit a hundred tramps in one night, and these are handled by a staff of at most three porters. A hundred ruffians could not be controlled by three unarmed men. Indeed, when one sees how tramps let themselves be bullied by the workhouse officials, it is obvious that they are the most docile, broken-spirited creatures imaginable. Or take the idea that all tramps are drunkards – an idea ridiculous on the face of it. No doubt many tramps would drink if they got the chance, but in the nature of things they cannot get the chance. At this moment a pale watery stuff called beer is sevenpence a pint in England. To be drunk on it would cost at least half a crown, and a man who can command half a crown at all often is not a tramp. The idea that tramps are impudent social parasites ('sturdy beggars') is not absolutely unfounded, but it is only true in a few per cent of the cases. Deliberate, cynical parasitism, such as one reads of in Jack London's books on American tramping, is not in the English character. The English are a conscience-ridden race, with a strong sense of the sinfulness of poverty. One cannot imagine the average English-man deliberately turning parasite, and this national character does not necessarily change because a man is thrown out of work. Indeed, if one remembers that a tramp is only an Englishman out of work, forced by law to live as a vagabond, then the tramp-monster vanishes. I am not saying, of course, that most tramps are ideal characters; I am only saying that they are ordinary human beings, and that if they are worse than other people it is the result and not the cause of their way of life.

---

Many people believe that, with the recession, the clock is being turned back. That is happening. But another pattern is also emerging, a new pattern, the pattern of youth homelessness. In this, heroin addiction replaces alcoholism; prostitution and petty street crime supplant low wages and casual jobs; and a nihilistic antagonism takes over from an apathetic cringing towards authority. Today's homeless youth, like the homeless of the thirties and their older compatriots on skid row, are unemployed. And many, after weeks of fruitless job-searching, no longer believe that employment is achievable. With the continuous massive de-skilling of many jobs and the waning of the work ethic, neither work nor the consumer benefits it can bring seems particularly desirable.

The only real imagination that is required today is to see homeless people as ordinary people. But, just as our skills have been stripped away from us, so, too, has our imagination. We cannot imagine any other state of affairs. We cannot see through our own and other people's stigmatization. We cannot recognize that the odd pieces of behaviour that some people show in one context are really no odder than other pieces of human behaviour – for instance, fox hunting – in other contexts. Imagination is required. So, too, is a sense of generosity. A generosity which stretches the limits of tolerance; a generosity which is the reverse of the current political climate, of the ethos of looking after number one, of self-interest and the fiddle.

Of course all this necessitates a new approach and responsibility towards housing provision, an overturning of the antiquated vagrancy laws and a stern defence of everyone's civil liberties. And somehow, also, we must frame and police a system which guarantees everyone a minimum wage, though that in itself will prove ineffective without other controls such as security of housing and fair rents. (Otherwise landlords will continue to raise rents and make money hand over fist out of the Welfare State.) Those are just a few of the things we must do, and if it puts up the cost of certain items, of rates, mortgage payments and luxury items, then it is still vastly preferable to the price in human misery and waste that the homeless are currently paying.

They are not homeless because they choose to be. Nor through any reasons of social or personal inadequacy or moral turpitude. They are homeless because of the specific workings of a specific social system which, at present, is not answering their needs. And we have schooled a generation in the belief that the glory of our society is the range of consumer choice it offers. We have trained this generation – and ourselves – to expect that life is about making those choices. That is their birthright. As part of the bargain, they have submerged their creativity. And then, with the recession, we have denied them those choices, prevented them assuaging their appetites. This is the generation who have come to London and found nothing. They are reflections – distorted, brutalized and more miserable – of ourselves. They are ordinary people.

*Eleven in the morning crashed out behind Les Halles.*

*Seven in the evening, pouring with rain outside, this homeless man lies exhausted in an entrance to St Michel metro (overleaf).*

PARIS

*Begging on St Germain* (opposite) *and in the metro* (this page). *These pathetic, hand-written life stories with their tales of eviction, marital break-up, release from prison and destitution are an increasingly common sight on the streets of Paris.*

PARIS

The First of May Demonstration, Place de la République: the process of alienation. Marching under their banner some of the out of work, homeless and marginalized youths of Paris (opposite) *tried to join in the demonstration, but were violently prevented by Communist stewards* (this page, above).

PARIS

*On the steps at the bottom of the Forum des Halles. This meeting point for punks, zonards, babacools and other disaffected youth is in the centre of one of Paris's plushest and busiest shopping piazzas. Their presence offends the passing window-shoppers and strolling bourgeoisie (this page).*

*Zonard and fourteen-year-old runaway girlfriend (opposite).*

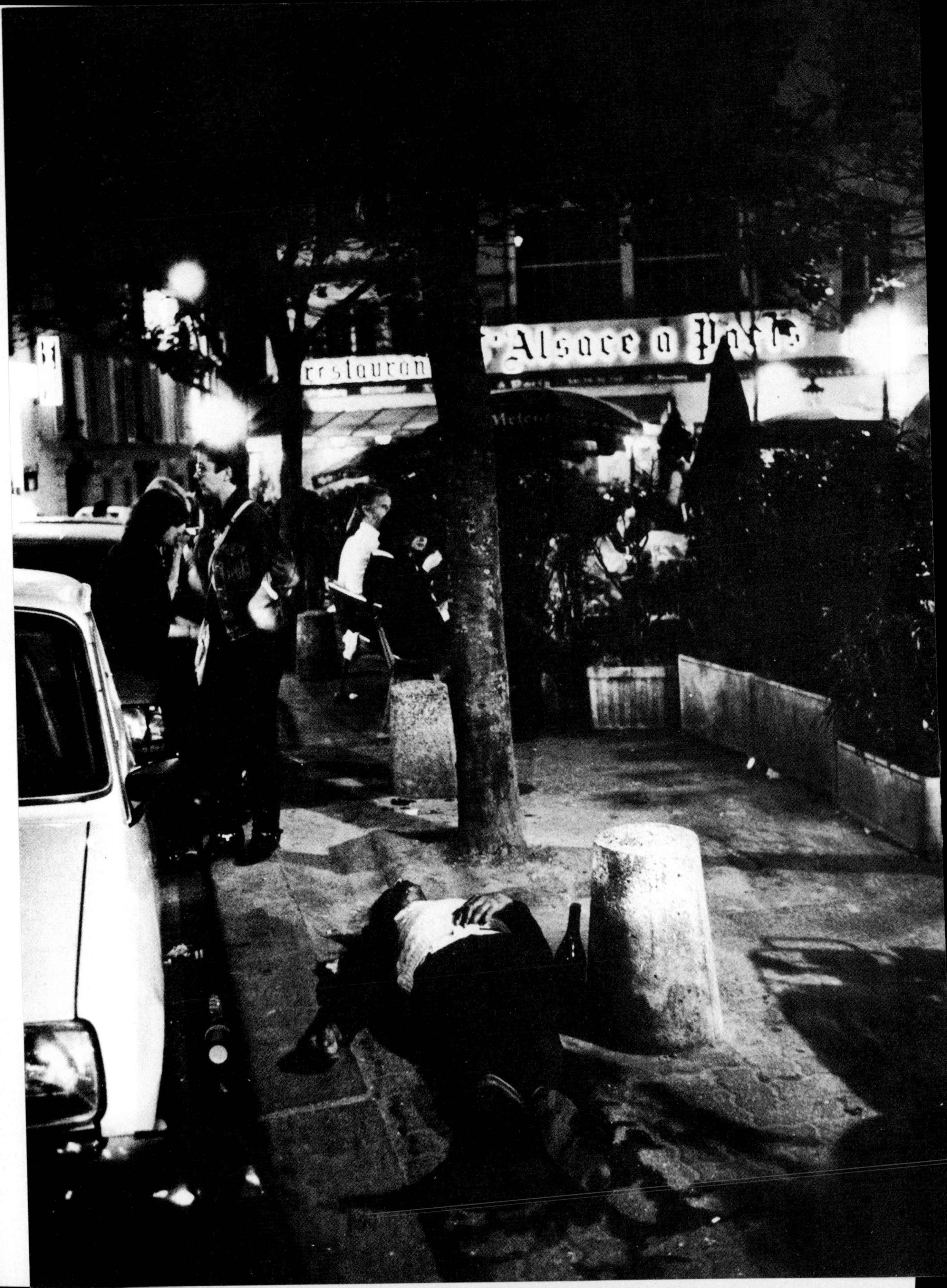
Alsace

*A forgotten immigrant lies in a drunken stupor on the Boulevard St Michel at midnight* (opposite).

Clochard *waiting to be taken to the 'Prison for the Hungry' – part prison, part public hospital, part workhouse – only the most desperate volunteer to go there* (this page).

PARIS

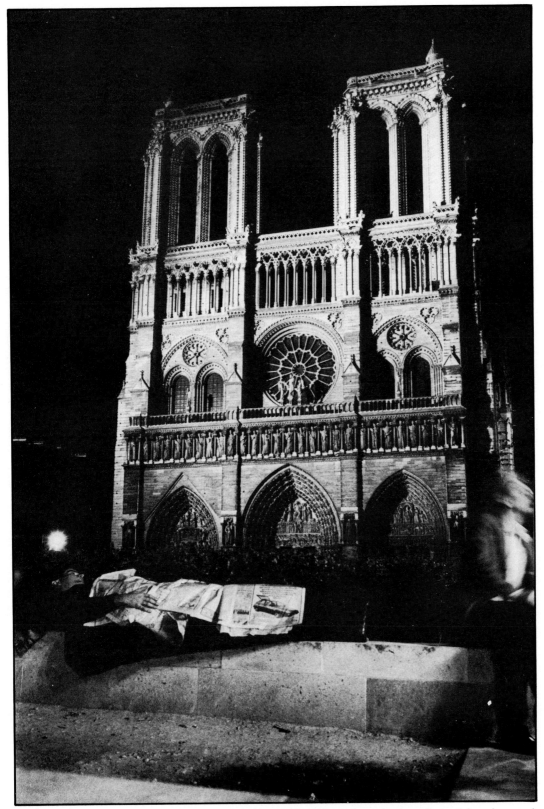

*The clochard sits hoping the occasional tourist will give him a franc* (opposite, above).
*Accidents are common, injuries slow to heal when living on the street* (opposite, below).

*After the tourist coaches have departed, homeless people sleep on the benches by Notre Dame* (this page).

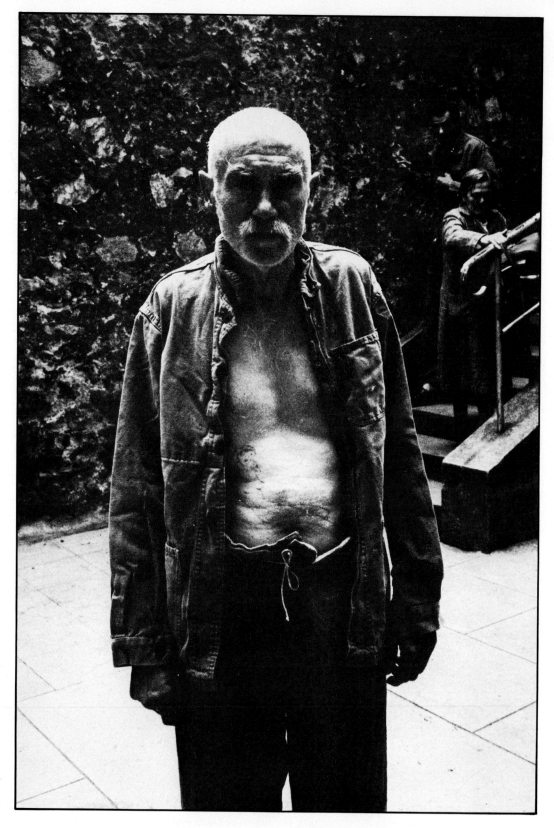

PARIS

Clochards *being picked up by* les bleus, *a special division of the police, on their daily round of parks and public spaces. Some* clochards *go quietly; others are caught by* les bleus *using pincer movements and similar military tactics.*

*His crime: to be poor and homeless. His punishment: to be taken to the 'Prison for the Hungry' where he will be compulsorily showered, deloused and made to wear the shabby regulation uniform. The authorities will now make his decision for him.*

PARIS

*Drop-outs under Pont Neuf. 'Instant' relationships, such as this one involving a newly arrived teenage German girl, are common.*

PARIS

*Parisians have adopted the older* clochard, *some of whom stay in the same neighbourhood for years* (opposite, below).
*They find it difficult to assimilate the younger, more threatening drop-outs* (opposite, above).

*Often, however, they ignore the down-and-out completely* (this page).

PARIS

*Early afternoon on a hot air grille in the quartier latin. This clochard remained undisturbed and ignored amidst the riots which raged around him later that week.*

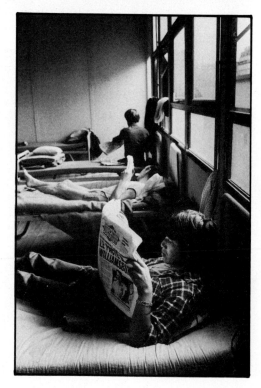

Last night of the Salvation Army's Emergency Night
Hostel at La Villette (below), yet there is no room for any
more beds on their barge moored at Quai d'Austerlitz.

PARIS    This Englishman had to leave the RAF, went to the Continent looking for work and was returning to England,
jobless and homeless (above).

*Rue de Rivoli, First of May. This clochard has been given lily of the valley, the traditional May Day flower (above).*

*Glue-sniffing on the steps of Les Halles, the zonards' own territory (below).*

PARIS

*Their private world. Babacools on the steps of Les Halles (left).*
*This group slept in a doorway of an unoccupied shop opposite the Pompidou Centre. The German on the right started 'travelling' in the late sixties and forget to stop (right).*

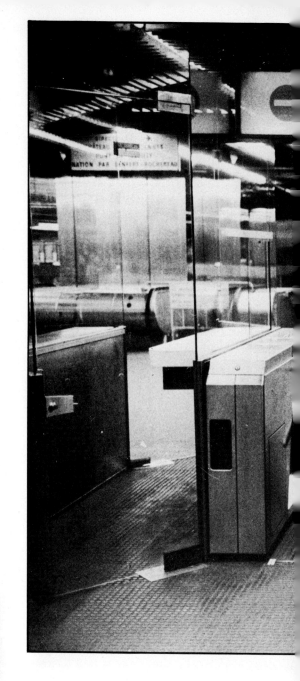

Zonards *never pay on the metro* (above).
*A non-architect-designed* pissoir *on the balcony above the*
*Forum de Halles. Behind the one-way glass classical*
*musicians were practising* (opposite).

*Under Pont Neuf. A clochard fell off the river wall here while asleep and drowned a few days before this photo-graph was taken. Now, with each new bottle of wine opened, his friends ritually pour some into the Seine in his memory (left).*

*Injured in a motor accident (his left leg is shorter than his right), he now ventures from his pitch under Pont Neuf only to beg on the bridge above and to buy food and wine from the local store (right).*

PARIS

*In a zonards' squat in Vincennes – this one had no electricity, water or other services and was apparently raided regularly by the police. Fortune-telling, drugs and wine help pass the time* (top and centre).
*Sharing a joint outside Les Halles* (below).

*Sewing a patch onto her jeans in the squat in Vincennes.*

PARIS

*The steps at Les Halles. The threatening behaviour, the occasional fight, glue-sniffing and constant bumming of cigarettes makes the steps a no-go area for the bourgeois Parisian.*

PARIS

*Whiling away the hours in the quartier latin* (above).
*Tattoos are often the secret symbols for ex-convicts, army*
*deserters or those who have been in care* (below).

*After midnight shopping near the Pompidou Centre. Her friends always send her to the all-night supermarket because she gets the best deal for the left-over bread (this page).*

*Mid-afternoon, Square des Innocents – another of the meeting points in the punks' aimless daily circuit. English bands, like the Sex Pistols and The Crass, are idolized, and the English punk scene idealized (overleaf).*

*Innocent and vulnerable, hanging around the steps at Les Halles* (opposite).

*Crab, named after his disfigured hand, enjoyed impressing his friends and play-acting with his pistol* (this page).

LONDON

*Derogatory terms used to describe homeless people:*
*dosser, vagrant, tramp, drifter, bum, hobo, beggar,*
*scrounger, parasite, sponger. Near Westminster Cathedral*
(this page). *In Deptford* (opposite).

LONDON

*Reading the Sunday paper, Bacon Street in the East End (opposite).*
*The morning after the night before, Camden Town (this page).*

LONDON

*Two a.m., all-night café, Whitehall. Depending on the manager's mood, one can take a couple of hours over drinking one cup of tea.*

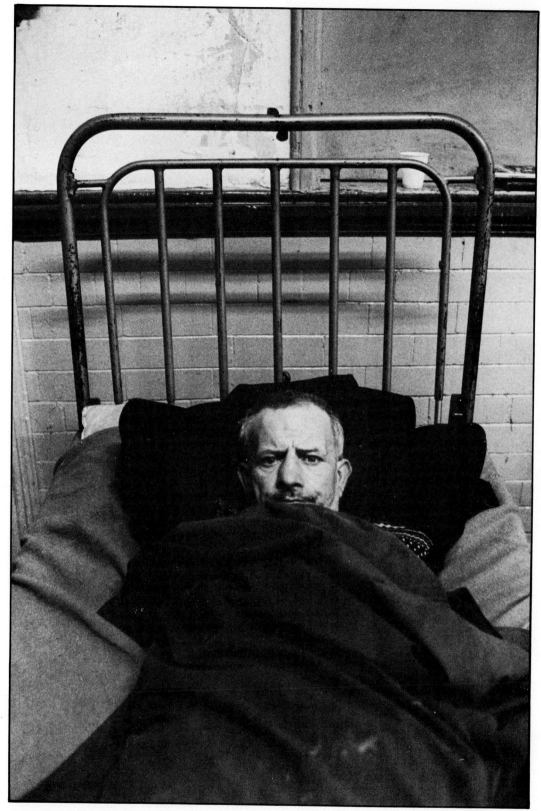

LONDON

*Manchester Night Shelter: a reminder that homelessness is
not confined to London.*

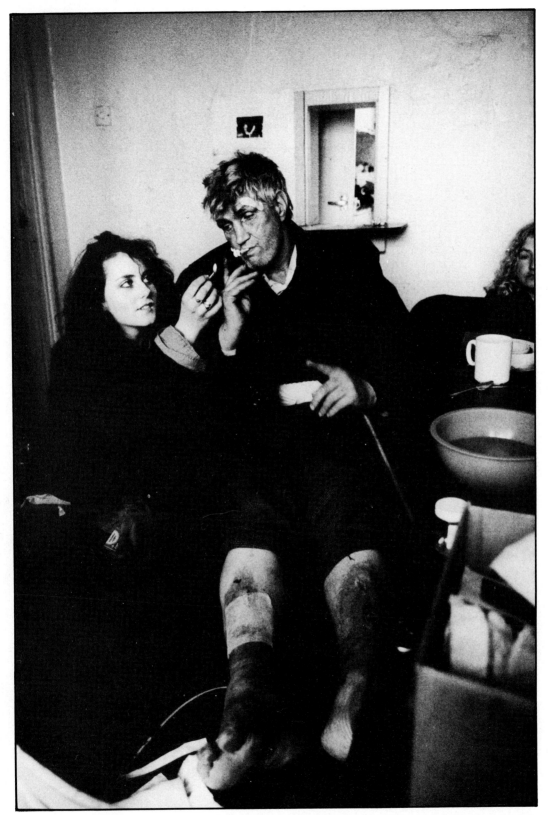

Simon Community Hostel, NW5: giving first aid for leg ulcers. This is one of a number of alcohol-related diseases from which this homeless man suffers. The ulcers are made worse by having to walk the streets and by the lack of any adequate public washing facilities. He drinks partly to dull the pain of the ulcers. There are few de-tox units to help break this cycle. Instead, however, he is used in a London teaching hospital as an example of alcohol-related diseases for the instruction of medical students.

LONDON

*Mortimer Street: the government's employment office for casual workers in the hotel and catering trade. Until recently this office opened at 6.45 a.m., when around one hundred men (and a few women) would be waiting in line.*

*Of these, some sixty men would have queued all night, sleeping in cardboard boxes discarded by local traders. When the office opened, the men shoved and fought to push their Social Security cards into the hands of the staff*

*through the crack between the doors. At 8.30 a.m. the lucky ones returned to be allocated a day's work portering or washing dishes for £1.20–£2 per hour. They have queued all night to fight for a day's pay. This system has now been changed, effectively preventing anyone working regularly.*

**LONDON**

*Booking Office, Salvation Army Hostel. It's very hard to book without money* (this page, above).
*Canteen/recreation room, Salvation Army Hostel: the limbo-land where many men live out their lives* (this page, below).

*St Mungo's Night Shelter in the old Charing Cross Hospital. This dosshouse is the 'home' of many ex-servicemen* (opposite).

LONDON

*Queueing for supper. Though this hostel was already overcrowded, others – less fortunate – were turned away (this page).*
*This Scot was swaying around Euston Station in the middle of the night, totally incapable – whether from drink or his injuries or both is impossible to say. The clamp helps the fractured skull knit together (opposite).*

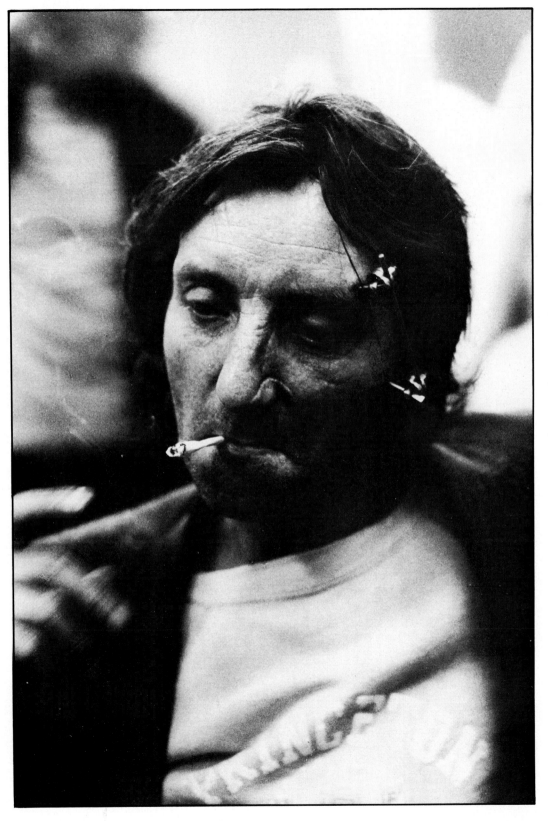

LONDON

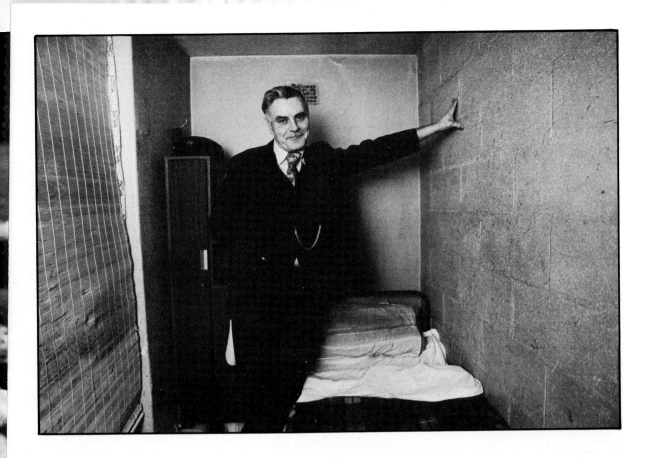

*Skippering in a condemned building near King's Cross.*
*His consumptive friend lying on a damp mattress in the*
*corner of the room did not want to be photographed*
*(opposite).*
*Dressed up and looking for work: a long-term resident of*
*Parker Street Hostel, Covent Garden (this page).*

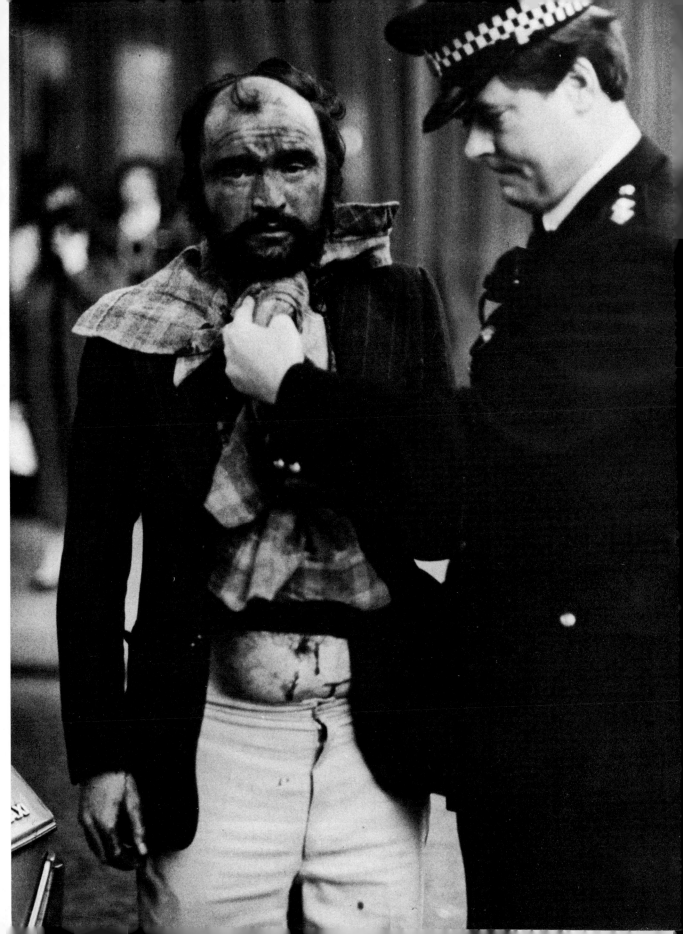

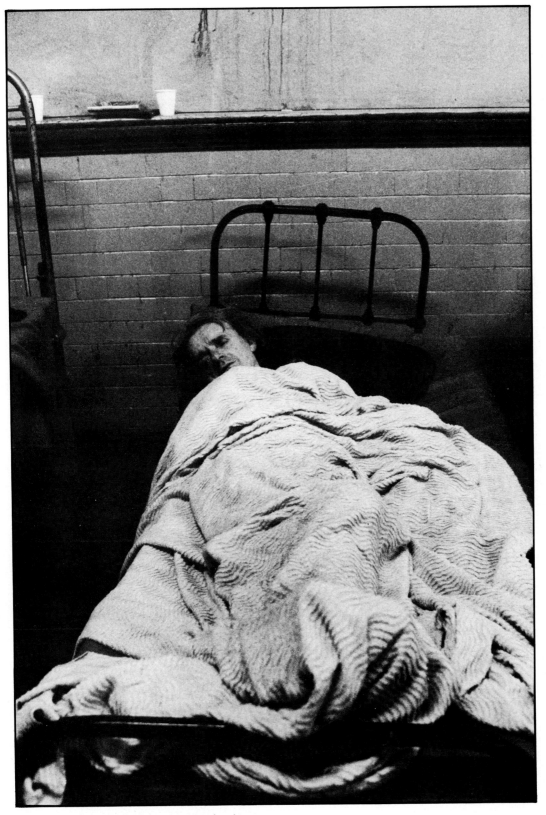

*Policeman applying a makeshift tourniquet after this man
got stabbed in the neck during a fight over a bottle of cider
(opposite).*
*Many at this hostel slept on the floor (this page).*

*Spitalfields Market. An ex-hostel dweller who now rents
his own room searches for waste food (this page).
After living for fifteen years in this 8 by 4 cubicle, Mr Good
has now moved into an old people's home (opposite).*

LONDON

*Homeless skinheads hanging around the West End. It is becoming increasingly difficult for voluntary agencies like Piccadilly Advice Centre to find a bed for young people homeless in the West End. The resources are shrinking (opposite).*

*Young people of unconventional appearance find it harder to secure both accommodation and work (this page).*

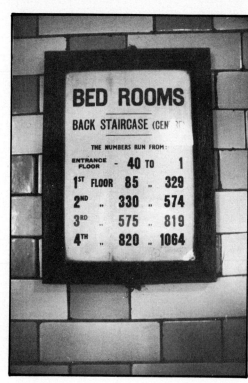

BED ROOMS

BACK STAIRCASE (CENTRE)

THE NUMBERS RUN FROM:

| ENTRANCE FLOOR | - | 40 | TO | 1 |
|---|---|---|---|---|
| 1ST FLOOR | 85 | „ | 329 |
| 2ND „ | 330 | „ | 574 |
| 3RD „ | 575 | „ | 819 |
| 4TH „ | 820 | „ | 1064 |

LONDON

*Arlington House, a typical Victorian hostel still in use today. The motto of its founder, Lord Rowton, was 'Philanthropy plus five per cent'. A member of the Arlington House Action Committee, who helped the staff unionize and fought successfully for the compulsory purchase of the hostel by the local council, in his 'cell': it was his twenty-first birthday.*

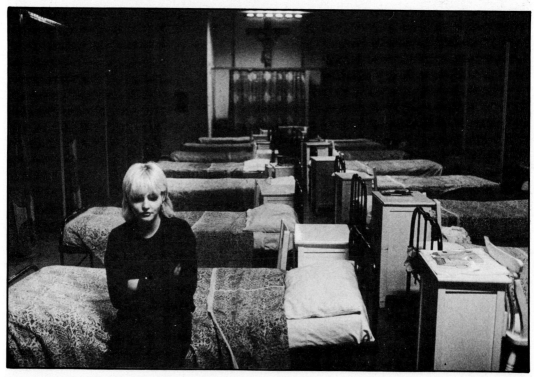

LONDON

Women's Section of Providence Row Night Refuge, Whitechapel: strict rules, no privacy, the ethos of charity. This was the temporary accommodation for this girl who, after her experiences in the West End, had decided to return home to Ireland (below).

Temporary squat in a tower-block estate, Elephant and Castle. Often the relationships are as temporary as the accommodation (above).

*Mixing up paste to dye his own and his friend's hair in a hotel bedroom* (this page).

*Wednesday afternoon, a bed-and-breakfast hotel, Earl's Court. This room became the unofficial social centre and crash pad for many of the area's disaffected youth* (overleaf).

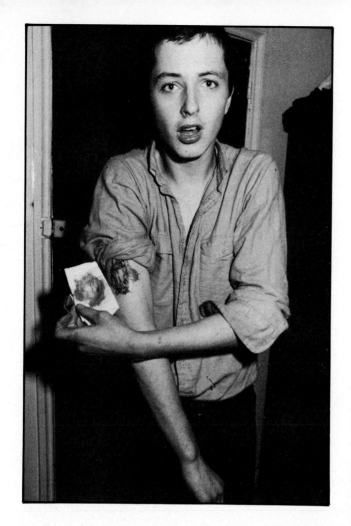

LONDON

*Petal, a regular of the all-night café scene: 'For a cup of tea, it's the cheapest night-club in London' (this page).*

*After paying for this tattoo, he had only three pounds of his Social Security money to last him the week (opposite).*

LONDON

*Living on a friend's floor in a one-room basement bedsit in Earl's Court. Early Saturday afternoon: getting up and ready to go down the King's Road.*

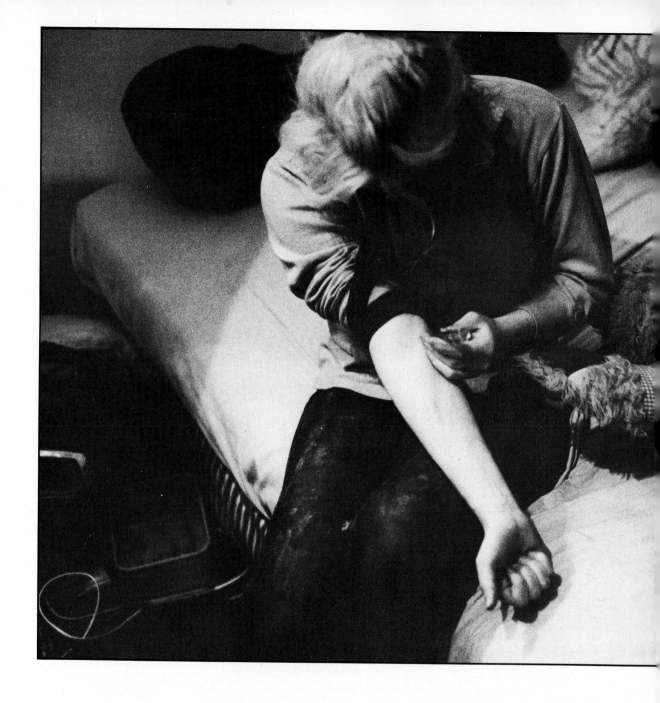

LONDON

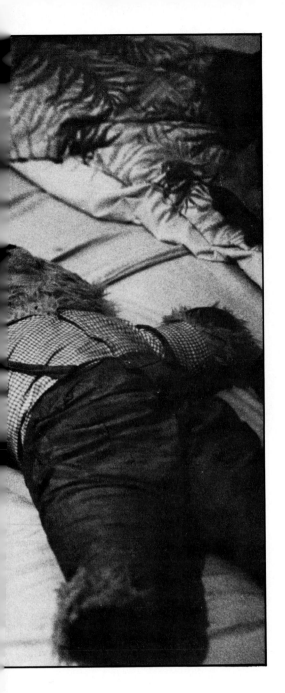

*'It's like on smack you feel totally together. Only trouble is you itch. And I don't know why it is, but I always puke up.' More and more young people are turning to heroin (opposite) and other drugs, including barbiturates (this page).*

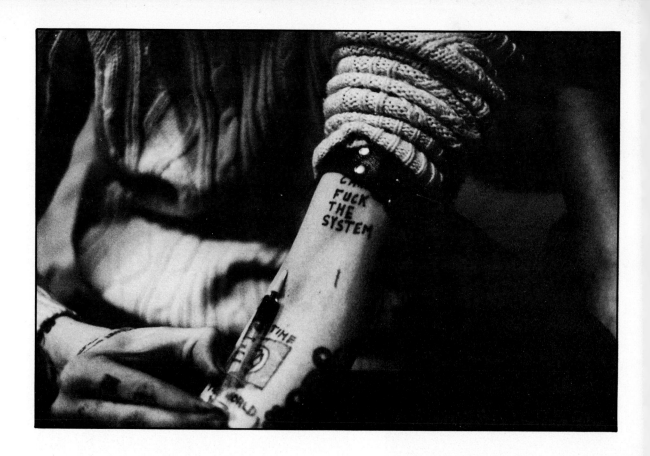

LONDON

The problems relating to the injection of heroin, such as hepatitis, and the adulteration of heroin, such as overdose, are more commonly found on the streets, not in the comfortable homes of wealthy users (this page).

'The Plaza Suite', Middlesex Hospital: emergency overnight stay for overdose cases. Though unwilling, the staff legally have to return any substances to the shaken users when they leave in the morning (opposite).

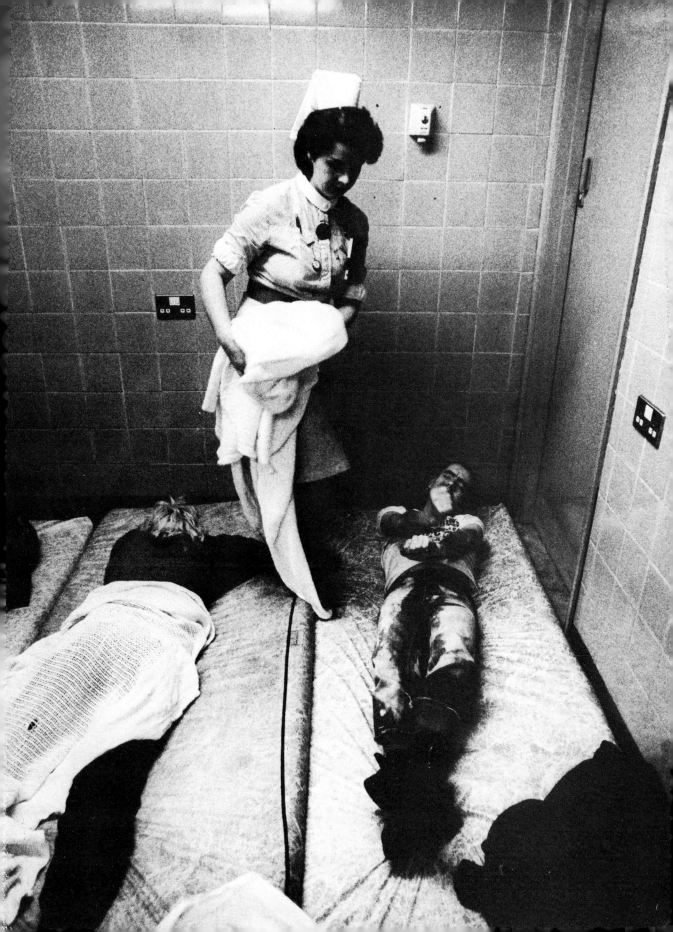